the bloomingdale's book of entertaining

Anne Bertsch

the bloomingdale's book of entertaining

ariane & michael batterberry

photographs by s. varnedoe

random house / new york

All rights reserved under International and Pan-American Copyright Conventions. Published in the United States by Random House, Inc., New York, and simultaneously in Canada by Random House of Canada Limited, Toronto.

Library of Congress Cataloging in Publication Data

Batterberry, Ariane Ruskin.
Bloomingdale's book of entertaining.

1. Entertaining. 2. Dinners and dining. 3. Menus. 4. Cookery, International. I. Batterberry, Michael, joint author. II. Bloomingdale Brothers, Inc., New York. III. Title.
TX731.B364   642'.41   76-16588
ISBN 0-394-40082-8

Grateful acknowledgment is made to the following for permission to reprint previously published material:

Coward, McCann & Geoghegan, Inc.: Menu for a "Gourmet Picnic" and recipe for "Ratatouille" from *Entertaining Menus* by Anne Willan. Copyright © 1974 by Anne Willan Cherniavsky.

Delacorte Press: Recipe for "Pâté de Campagne, Provençale" excerpted from *Menus for Entertaining* by James Beard. Copyright © 1965 by James Beard.

Alfred A. Knopf, Inc.: Recipes for "Cucumber and Tomato with Lemon Juice" and "Marinated Broiled Chicken" from *An Invitation to Indian Cooking* by Madhur Jaffrey. Copyright © 1973 by Madhur Jaffrey.

Little, Brown and Company: Excerpts from *How to Do It* by Elsa Maxwell.

Random House, Inc.: Recipes for "Chicken Liver Pâté" and "Baked Ham with Apricot Glaze" from *Cooking With Helen McCully Beside You* by Helen McCully. Copyright © 1970 by Helen McCully.

Ruth A. Spear: Recipes for "Fresh Raspberry Pie," "Barbequed Marinated Leg of Lamb," "Stuffed Breast of Veal," "Striped Bass Baked with Mussels and Shrimp," "Rice Salad," and "Chilled Pea and Lettuce Soup" from *The Easthampton Cookbook* by Ruth A. Spear.

The Viking Press, Inc.: Recipes for "Geoffrey's Snake Bite (Rum Punch)" and "Bulljoul" from *Geoffrey Holder's Caribbean Cookbook* by Geoffrey Holder. Copyright © 1973 by Geoffrey Holder.

Designed by Antonina Krass

Manufactured in the United States of America
2 3 4 5 6 7 8 9
First Edition

contents

a note from bloomingdale's

We believe that Bloomingdale's is more than a store—rather, it is an attitude. And that attitude is style. Whether it's the latest looks from St. Tropez, the newest cinnabar jewelry from China, how to wrap a scarf, tie a bow or serve sushi for fourteen, Bloomingdale's represents a way of living. It is vivacious yet classic, amusing without losing a serious concern for excellence. It is the essence of style.

Part of the joy of living well is entertaining. And entertaining with style is part of the Bloomingdale mystique. This book contains ideas, suggestions, secrets, menus, recipes, table settings, formulas—the do's and don't's and concepts on fashionable entertaining—from people whose creative and original approach to entertaining is characteristic of the Bloomingdale attitude.

These "Bloomingdale People," many of whom you know, were chosen because they view home entertaining as an integral part of an original life-style. Taking you into their homes to see how they entertain should, we hope, offer inspiration to all who would become hosts par excellence.

You might wonder how Bloomingdale's expertise in entertaining came about. Beginning with basic dining, we have seven full-service restaurants, ten employee cafeterias, four snack shops, four "Forty Carrots" health food bars. And on a more lavish scale, our Delicacies Department imports specialties from every country of Europe, as well as twenty-two other countries around the world. In our Bread Basket, no fewer than a hundred forty different kinds of bread are created every day. Our salads, pâtés, cheeses and Cornet chocolates are legendary. And our exotic gourmet food—Himalayan ice cream prepared from fresh Indian mangoes or papayas, the best green peppercorns for perfect steak au poivre, thirty varieties of tea, and the choicest escargots this side of France—are often that exquisite touch which makes a dinner party memorable.

On the technical side of entertaining, we carry cookware from all over the world. Recently we developed our own Cooks' Kitchen, a collection of the best and the basic in kitchen equipment and utensils, selected from the *Cooks' Catalog* by James Beard, Milton Glaser and Burton Wolf. Our fine China, Glass and Silver Departments provide the widest variety of beautiful and functional table settings for formal and informal entertaining.

On the subject of parties we are expert. We have been hosts, on separate occasions, to Prince Philip, Queen Elizabeth II, the mayors of New York, Boston, Philadelphia and Washington. We have entertained stars of stage, screen and television. We have even entertained that most discriminating group of guests, the culinary artists of international fame. We have held countless wine-tastings, afternoon teas, children's parties, dances, brunches, breakfasts, formals, informals, block parties and barbeques. And our greatest party we gave for ourselves. When we arrived at the ripe old age of one hundred, we hosted the "Party of the Century," a black tie, five-course, sit-down pheasant dinner for 1300 guests. And we held the party on the eighth floor of our 59th Street Store. The logistics involved defy description, and were rivaled by nothing less than a coronation ball. But few were the wine stains, and we were back in business on that floor the following morning. For the Wine & Food Society, we held a progressive dinner throughout our 59th Street Store. Called "Great Caterers Meet Great Hostesses," the party began in the Book Stalls on the seventh floor with champagne and *seviche* and concluded with a candlelight pastry extravaganza in the Delicacies Department.

No effort is spared in making sure that our entertainments entertain. We thought you would want to know about the Bloomingdale approach to entertaining and to see how some of the "Bloomingdale People" do it.

Peggy Healy
Mary Baumslag

the past

America has always loved a party. With unflagging enthusiasm, we have given and gone to barn dances and masquerades, debutante teas and barbecues, ice cream socials and cocktail parties, hoedowns and poker games, clambakes and ladies' lunches, kaffeeklatsches and twelve-course banquets, covered dish suppers and quilting bees, not to mention christenings, engagements, weddings and wakes. For foreign visitors, American hospitality has become a synonym for spontaneous generosity and warmth. As a nation, we have been described as the melting pot, and rightly so; nowhere are the lingering charms of our mixed heritage more vividly shown than in the way we entertain. But while our styles may vary, particularly today when social self-expression is considered a birthright, our traditional impulse to enjoy the company of others under our own roofs remains unshaken.

Although George Washington may be known as the father of our country, by no stretch of the imagination would he be named the presidential sire of American entertaining. On the surface, he followed the traditional rules of Southern plantation hospitality and generosity and looked to the able assistance of his steward Sam Fraunces, who insisted that the presidential table be "bountiful and elegant." But something was amiss.

3

The great man had no small talk. William Maclay, Senator from Pennsylvania, recalled a presidential dinner in which the dining room was overheated. The food was fine enough, although the menu leaned almost exclusively to protein and sweets, in the eighteenth-century English fashion: game soup; fish, roasted and boiled, joints, gammon and fowls, followed by apple pies, puddings, ice creams, jellies, watermelons, musk melons, apples, peaches and nuts. "But the President is a cold, formal man," reported Maclay. "Not a health drank, scarce a word said, until the cloth was taken away." Then Washington toasted the health of each guest, and everyone followed suit, but apart from this, "there was a dead silence, almost." When the ladies withdrew, poor Maclay's hopes momentarily rose—"but the same stillness remained." Finally, as his guests waited in rapt attention, a witicism came to the President's lips: "The President told of a New England clergyman who had lost a hat and wig in passing a river called the Brunks..."

Thomas Jefferson, on the other hand, was the kind of host we all understand and admire. He liked to sit down to dinner with twelve to fourteen friends and to stay up talking half the night. His overseer at Monticello claimed that his "guests arrived in gangs," and "almost ate him out of house and home." Washington had said, "My manner of living is plain and I do not mean to be put out by it. A glass of wine and a bit of mutton are always welcome." Jefferson's manner, on the other hand, was not plain at all. His years in France had made him a gourmet. He brought home from European tables Parmesan cheese, Calcutta hogs, Dutch waffles, a form of potato now called "French fries," a new recipe for ice cream, and an invention called "Baked Alaska."

Once ensconced in the White House, Jefferson stunned the public with an avant-garde combination of "Republican convictions and Epicurean tastes." He continued to enjoy small suppers and tête-à-têtes. He was the first President to shake hands with his guests, and he went in to dinner on the arm of whichever lady stood nearest him. (In the early days of the Republic, any visitor to Washington who was properly dressed might expect to wangle a White House invitation.) Moreover, unlike Washington, who always stood in velvet breeches, with his cocked hat under his arm, Jefferson was simply dressed. He finally succeeded in scandalizing the British Ambassador and his wife by greeting them in his carpet slippers.

Jefferson's table, which was round to avoid seating by rank, was famously well appointed. He returned from France with a French chef and a taste for daubes, ragouts and soufflés quite at variance with the unadorned "boil and roast" concepts of English cookery to which most Americans still cling. He also possessed a cultivated taste for French vintage wines and champagnes, on which he spent no less than $3,000 (a monumental sum in his day) in a single year. Patrick Henry harangued that the President had

The Flax Scutching Bee, Linton Park

"adjured his native victuals," and John Adams primly sniffed, "Jefferson's whole eight years was a levee."

The more sophisticated men and women of the Revolutionary period, like aristocrats of eighteenth-century Europe, frequently followed dinner with a brisk game of cards; "Quadrille" and "Ombre" were the favorites of the day. They also enjoyed assemblies, theater galas, fox hunts and sleighing parties. But in the rural areas of America and on the frontier, life was very different. There, social gatherings, even if held in one family's house, might include the entire community. Parties often had a constructive purpose: quilting bees, haying, berrying, house-raising, corn-husking and apple-picking parties, all in effect indoor and outdoor picnics. In the winter, there were skating and sledding parties, climaxed by a steaming hot toddy at someone's home.

The holidays most celebrated were not those one might expect. New Englanders, except for the inhabitants of Anglican Rhode Island, shunned Christmas, although Southerners celebrated it as warmly as the English themselves. Thanksgiving was the great national holiday. It fell on almost any day from October to December, until it was finally

5

designated by Washington as an official holiday to be celebrated on the third Thursday in November. Turkey appeared on every Thanksgiving—the colonists' answer to the "beef of old England."

At the time of the Revolution and for years after, dancing was a kind of mania throughout the United States, so much so that the church relaxed its prohibitions. Dancing was taught in towns, large and small, by teachers who were stationary or itinerant. Any social group that included a fiddler, in private or in public, was apt to lapse into the popular "contredances": "The Orange Tree" or "Old Father George." The French statesman Chateaubriand reported once wandering through the primeval north woods of New York searching for "men in their true and natural state" (Indians). What he found was a band of Iroquois learning the latest Parisian steps from a deserter of Rochambeau's army, fiddling away in the unsullied air and making a fortune in pelts as dancing master to the tribe.

Dining and entertaining in nineteenth-century America apparently were of a style uniquely ours—and that style was frequently criticized by foreign travelers, particularly the English. At a ball in the South one British visitor pronounced the women overdressed and their dancing inelegant. He heartlessly sneered at the American habit of mixing ages, with very old women, very young ones and children all invited together. Mrs. Trollope, mother of the novelist, stopping in the Midwest in the 1830's, commented on the Americans' "frightful manner of feeding with their knives, til the whole blade seemed to enter the mouth, and still more frightful manner of cleaning the teeth after with a pocket knife." Americans, it was noted, might turn tea or coffee from the cup to cool in the saucer, lean on the table, or use the cloth for anything, including the blowing of the nose. Moreover, they devoured enormous meals in a matter of ten or fifteen minutes from beginning to end. One irascible Englishman pronounced: "Civilty cannot be purchased from them on any terms. They seem to think that it is incompatible with freedom."

Americans were, in fact, anxious to purchase civilty, in the form of books on etiquette. Already vastly popular in England, etiquette books became so much the rage in America that by the 1830's sales of titles such as *The Habits of Good Society* and *Manners—How They Can Be Acquired* began to overtake the Bible. The American etiquette books differed in one basic respect from their English prototypes. Whereas the English books instructed the reader that it was not respectable to attempt to rise above one's station, Americans would have no truck with the very idea of station, and would not have bought the books if they didn't have every intention of rising. Etiquette books were of great importance because in America it was behavior, not birth, which defined position. All were created equal, but after that, etiquette book in hand, the race was on.

At first, many of the etiquette books were written in a tone that might have been confused with holy writ. In his *Principles of Courtesy with Hints and Observations* (published in 1852) George Winfred Hervey exhorts the hostess with references to the hospitality of Abraham, Sarah, Lot and Boaz, and advises her "not to boast distinguished and far famed guests," but rather "entertain some angel unawares." Getting down to practicalities, he suggests that when guests are assembled a servant or some member of the family should announce that dinner is served, and that the master or mistress then lead the way, with each gentleman taking the arm of a lady of similar age or "rank." The hostess should make a point of seeing to it that relatives or persons of the same profession do not sit together. At the table there is to be no loud blowing, chewing, sucking or sipping, or discussion of food. "Feed yourself with a fork or a spoon, not with a knife." Moreover, "Our organs are so formed that we cannot speak and eat well at the same time." Hervey also suggests that if the group is small the guests should be allowed to carve and help themselves, dispensing with servants: "It would thin those troublesome retinues of household servants, which could have been necessary or proper only in feudal times."

When Mr. Hervey speaks of guests helping themselves, he is referring to the old-fashioned custom of serving dinner in two "courses," with all the dishes of each plunked down on the simple white cloth of the table at once: for the first course, soup, fish, meat, game and vegetable dishes would be set out; for the second, puddings, tarts, cakes, ices, cheeses and fruits. Later, service *à la Russe* was introduced. This meant that food was no longer placed on the table, but carved and served from a sideboard by waiters who offered each guest every dish in turn. Moreover, the hour of the dinner in question was changing even as Hervey wrote. Early in the nineteenth century, the main meal of the day, a very heavy one, was consumed at mid-afternoon. Evening entertainments might feature a late supper of cakes, meats, pickles and preserves. By mid-century the dinner hour had moved to six, and lunch was taking on the proportion of a modest but proper meal. It was not until the end of the century that formal dinners settled down to eight o'clock in the evening.

Mr. Hervey also mentions servants, and this was a touchy matter with Americans. In the nineteenth century, with wave upon wave of immigration, servants were available in the Eastern United States, although difficult to find farther west. But the American spirit of equality was against even the term "servant." Except in the slaveholding South, housewives were assisted by "help." The wearing of "livery" was out of the question.

Hervey, as we have seen, felt that by mid-century the "troublesome retinues" of servants were going out of style, along with overeating and drinking. "Among people of fashion free eating and drinking are passing out of favor; and the time is passed when a gentleman . . . must evince the devotedness of his friendship by tumbling down under the table in oblivious drunkenness."

Hervey was wrong. Within thirty years of his writing the great mansions of the Eastern seaboard were served by flocks of liveried servants, and guests were dining on meals that would beggar both his and our own imagination for sheer size. The reason for this extraordinary development was the growth of huge private fortunes at the time of the Civil War and shortly thereafter. For every millionaire in America in 1852, there were ten a generation or so later.

Mrs. John Sherwood, author of *A Transplanted Rose,* presents in the frontispiece of her book *Manners and Social Usages,* a picture entitled "The Modern Dinner Table." This is the dinner table of 1888, and it virtually disappears under a display of epergnes, bonbonnières, baskets, carafes, candelabra and a funereal mass of flowers. The mistress is told to instruct the butler, who is to instruct the footmen in proper arrangement of each setting: two knives, three forks and a soup spoon, a silver salt cellar, water carafe, napkin, menu and name card at each "cover," along with a water goblet, two champagne glasses, a Bohemian green glass for hock, a ruby red glass for claret, and two large clear Burgundy glasses. The footmen will wipe everything with a clean towel "so that no dampness of his own hand shall mar their sparkling cleanliness."

This is only the beginning. "As dinner goes on the guest revels in unexpected surprises in the beauty of the plates, some of which look as if made of solid gold; and when the Roman punch [a sherbet] is served it comes in the heart of a red, red rose, or in the bosom of a swan, or the cup of a lily . . ." Mrs. Sherwood's tips were expected to appeal to a large audience—at least large enough to support the sale of her book.

The meal served on such a table was as elaborate as its setting. In his autobiography, Ward McAllister, a bon vivant of the period, describes a meal in which he advises, for the soup course, a light *Tortue claire,* followed by *petites bouchées* in the form of a ham mousse. For the fish course, he counsels terrapin, and for the *relève,* if women are present, he will countenance nothing coarser than a fillet of beef with truffles. This is to be followed by the *entrées,* of which "two hot and one cold is sufficient," and he advises that, to provide a contrast to the dark sauce of the beef, one might serve a *suprème de volaille,* along with a pâté de foie gras and a hot vegetable, such as asparagus in Hollandaise sauce. "Then your *sorbet,* known in France as *la surprise,* as it is an ice, and produces on the mind the effect that the dinner is finished, when the grandest dish of the dinner makes its appearance in the shape of the roast canvasbacks, woodcock, snipe, or truffled capons, with salad." The salad, which may consist of mixed vegetables, is accompanied by camembert cheese and biscuits. The French, says McAllister, always give a hot pudding, but he omits this course and proceeds directly to the ices: "The fashion is now to make them very ornamental, a cornucopia for instance, but I prefer a *pouding Nesselrode.*" The entire is to be washed down with a succession of champagnes and wines, fortified and unfortified, and no more than one hour and a half is to be spent at table. McAllister warns, with only half a grain of salt, that an accepted invitation amounted to an almost religious duty, and if the guest died in the interim, his executor was beholden to attend the dinner.

Stiff, inhibited, exaggerated—formal entertaining in the Grand Manner was all of these. But Edith Wharton's memories give warmth to the icy dictates of the etiquette books: "I remember a mild blur of rosy and white-whiskered gentlemen, of ladies with bare sloping shoulders rising flower-like from voluminous skirts.... A great sense of leisure emanated from their kindly faces and voices.... There being no haste, and a prodigious amount of good food to be disposed of, the guests sat long at table; and when my mother bowed slightly ... and flounces and trains floated up the red velvet stair-carpet to the white-and-gold drawingroom with tufted purple satin arm chairs and voluminous purple satin curtains festooned with buttercup yellow fringe, the gentlemen settled down again to claret and Madeira, sent duly westward, and followed by coffee and Havana cigars.... Small parochial concerns no doubt formed the staple of the talk. Art and music and literature were rather timorously avoided ... and the topics chiefly dwelt on were personal: the thoughtful discussion of food, wine, horses ... the laying out and planting of country seats, the selection of specimen copper beeches ... and those plans of European travel that filled so large a space in the thought of old New Yorkers."

Dinners were not the only forms of home entertainment popular with Society in the larger cities. There were also mammoth luncheons, matinées ("at which artist and aristocrat can mix," according to Mrs. Sherwood), soirées with a touch of music or a bit of reading. Only the grandest houses could cope with balls, and most were held in the public rooms of establishments such as Delmonico's in New York.

But while wealthy Eastern families were enjoying "a great sense of leisure" as well as magnificence, on the American frontier neighbors still gathered in the frosty night for spicy yellow pumpkin pie, steaming golden donuts, and the sound of a fiddler at apple-paring and corn-husking bees. Meanwhile, in towns and small cities, in the Middle West, another tradition of entertaining had taken shape.

Mrs. Trollope, who lived briefly in Cincinnati in the 1830's, recalls an evening's "entertainment" with some venom: "The women invariably herd together at one part of the room, and the men at the other. ... Sometimes a small attempt at music produces a partial reunion. . . . The gentlemen spit, talk of elections and the price of produce, and spit again. The ladies look at each other's dresses till they know every pin by heart; talk of Parson Somebody's last sermon on the day of judgment, on Dr. T'otherbody's new pills for dyspepsia, till the "tea" is announced, when they all console themselves for whatever they may have suffered in keeping awake, by taking more tea, coffee, hot cake and custard, hoe cake, johnny cake, waffle cake, and dodger cake, pickled peaches, and preserved cucumbers, ham, turkey, hung beef, apple sauce, and pickled oysters than ever were prepared in any other country of the known world."

Mrs. Trollope is being grossly unfair. She disliked a good deal about America, specifically its egalitarian principles, which failed to set her above the mass of the Americans

A Welsh-Rarebit after the Theatre

THE PICTURE DECORATOR

she met, and she was in a permanent snit. What she in fact described came later in the century to be called a "lap-supper," the glory and delight of the Middle West and much of America. It remains important today and is, of course, now called a "buffet." The "lap-supper" evolved into many types: the Pound Party, the Shower, the Housewarming, the Infair, following a wedding. In rural areas it might take the form of a "covered dish" supper, to which each guest contributed.

Where distances were long, visitors came to stay, and to eat. Sarah S. Pratt, wife of a publisher, describes Indiana in the last half of the nineteenth century: "The style of entertainment called a party was of epidemic nature then. Perhaps it has always been so. Weeks of social quietude would be broken by someone's having a party. This was the outbreak, the preliminary rash of the party epidemic.

"These hostesses vied with each other in the supper which was called a lap-supper and was an elaborate feast. When Mrs. Bringhurst, who hated food, ventured early in the seventies to serve only coffee, cake and ices at her party, and to introduce a guessing game, society took sides in discussing it; the people who liked to guess, approved the innovation; the people who liked to eat, condemned it, and I think the latter carried the day."

Food was the chief concern. The chief worry: "If you don't have your party soon, the celery will be gone, and what will you do for chicken-salad?" Sugar had been in short supply during the Civil War, and after the War, the reaction, in the words of Mrs. Pratt, "took the form of gastronomic indulgence in which cake was supreme."

There is no denying it. During the years after the Civil War, the country as a whole, and the Middle West in particular, underwent what might be called the Great Cake Mania. Pound cake took pride of place—rich and eternally moist with a "pound" of butter, sugar, eggs, brandy. But there were others: marble cake, chocolate cake, jelly cake, black cake (fruit cake), gold cake, silver cake, coconut cake. New cakes were devised. The first was Angel's Food, which was approached with nothing less than awe. Recipes, techniques, tricks for achieving "Angel cake" were whispered, guessed at, bartered. "Angel's Food consumed fifteen egg whites." "It must be baked in a brand new pan, ungreased." "No one must walk in the kitchen while it is baking." "The oven door must not jar it." Just as Angel's Food was about to be accepted as commonplace, the Chicago Exposition brought the attention of the world to chocolate, and Devil's Food became the challenge. Chocolate Menier ("or manure, as it was artlessly called by some women"), was put to use in a hundred new ways, including the chocolate drop cookie. At the height of the cake fever, a hostess might serve twenty varieties of cake, and expect her guests to sample every one.

As they still do, Americans of the nineteenth century lived and entertained a good deal out-of-doors. This might mean anything from a simple family outing to a fantasy from the fevered imagination of Ward McAllister who, for a "country picnic" would hire a flock of sheep, a few yokes of cattle and several cows to decorate his fields for the day. But even McAllister indulged in the good American tradition of the covered dish supper. He invited his friends to bring the dishes for which their cooks were best known. Meanwhile, on the Western frontier, where the livestock was more than decorative, friends gathered around a pit or bonfire for a barbecue. The notion of joining together to devour a roasted animal is certainly the oldest known form of entertaining, but in the American West the technique was carried to the level of art and admired as such. William Allen White wrote: "Barbecue is any four footed animal—be it mouse or mastodon—whose dressed carcass is roasted whole . . . at its best it is a fat steer, and it must be eaten within an hour of when it is cooked. For if ever the sun rises upon Barbecue, its flavor vanishes like Cinderella's silks, and it becomes cold baked beef—staler in the chill dawn than illicit love."

As we moved into the twentieth century, there were many changes. War accustomed Americans to eating less. Moreover, women, active in the war, became active, even athletic in peace, and no longer yearned for the languorous curves of an earlier era. Men no longer sought the eminence of a pot belly. There was no way to reconcile the ten-course dinner or the twenty-cake supper with the flappers' desire for a flat-chested and elongated line. The newly exposed leg could not be allowed to balloon gracelessly. Moreover, the Grand Manner, taught so diligently by the etiquette books, died as soon as it was achieved—to everyone's relief. The growth of industry, the change in the status of women, and the slackening in immigration all contributed to exacerbating the problem always present in America—the shortage of servants in a country that had never had a "servant class."

The "niceties" and prejudices of tracts like Mrs. Sherwood's were against the spirit of the times. Her place was taken by Emily Post, who taught that an informal dinner consisting of soup, fish, roast, salad, dessert and coffee was acceptable, and so was a table covered with a simple white cloth, a centerpiece and four candlesticks. Meanwhile "lap-suppers" had become "buffets," and Mrs. Post was teaching her followers that a "stand-up lunch" was a "jolly sort of party." The barbecue moved from the range to the backyard, and it was no longer necessary to roast the whole animal. The American desire for instruction had collided with the American desire for freedom, the generosity of the frontier. Freedom won.

Elsa Maxwell was probably among the first celebrities to popularize the dizzy and careless new informality of the post World War I years. Her treasure hunts, her Hollywood cooking parties, her Barnyard Party at which guests in the costume of farmers and milkmaids plucked real apples from imitation trees, milked wooden cows for champagne and fled a stampede of live hogs, may seem as elaborate as McAllister's picnics, but a new feeling of relaxed informality made them fun. Elsa wanted to appeal to everyone's secret yearning: "Make me a child again, just for tonight." She took the offensive against the outdated etiquette Americans had once admired and were now ready to reject: "I declare war . . . on the etiquette that ordains a fixed, inflexible pattern of the way this or that party must be given—the etiquette that states, for example, that hot breads may *never* be served at a tea where there is dancing, that before a dinner the hostess *must* remain standing. . . . that when the guest of honor leaves *all* must leave." "What should a party be, in heaven's name?" boomed Elsa, "A good time, or an exercise in discipline?" (From Elsa Maxwell, *How To Do It,* published by Little, Brown and Co., Boston.)

the present

by the 1960's and 70's the last vestiges of rigid convention and etiquette, along with confining corsets and stiff starched shirts, were laughed away by most Americans. The result is a modern mood of ease and informality, comfort and practicality. But most important, it is a mood of personal freedom. We are no longer willing to lead stereotyped lives, to meekly obey dull laws passed down by self-appointed experts on doing "the correct thing." A demand for self-expression and creative style has carried the day.

Gratefully, joyfully, triumphantly, we have entered the age of the liberated host and hostess. Tribal taboos have been smashed. Men cook. Women choose wines, mix drinks and carve. No more do we have to think in stifling terms such as "bridge luncheon" or "formal dinner," each dictating its own strict set of rules. The same liberating gust of fresh air has fanned a passion for quality, whether in the choice of friends, food or furnishings. There is more confidence in personal values and personal taste. People no longer seem content to slip on their social masks and dutifully follow the rules. If a single phrase had to be chosen, "natural elegance" might sum up the new ideal in entertaining. But what precisely does natural elegance mean? How can it be achieved?

To answer these questions, we've interviewed a fascinating cross-section of talented hosts and hostesses, each of whom holds strong opinions about the meaning of entertaining well. As you read, you will find that as their backgrounds, tastes, budgets and ages vary widely, their ideas also occasionally fall into sharp conflict. Still, a strong common bond unites them all—a determination to be themselves which has led each to develop what might be called his true Entertaining Identity, the essential key to any host's success.

How can you learn from their example? First of all, decide what your own tastes are, deliberately casting out the old ideas of what entertaining should be. Put yourself through an honest session of self-scrutiny. What is it you really like and want? Other than gathering together good friends for mutual pleasure, have you a specific purpose for entertaining? To matchmake? To advance business or civic projects? To widen your circle and interests? To bask in admiration? One single woman we know is utterly frank: "I've designed my home as a stage, as a background for me—it's the place where I perform best." To achieve the effect she wants, she employs a subtle scheme which includes color coordinating her wardrobe and surroundings, right down to the last napkin, in shades which flatter her most. The trick, of course, is carrying it off so craftily that no one is aware of her wiles. This she accomplishes with a smoke screen of comfort—"Even *I* have to look comfortable. Before I buy a dress, I sit and lie in it to be sure. The same with the furniture; it must be comfortable for everyone, which in turn makes *me* feel and look good." Clearly this is a hostess who has found her own Entertaining Identity.

When singling out your own Entertaining Identity, consider: Are you more naturally oriented toward family, friends or career? Do you nurse a secret mad desire to start your own salon? Again, the point is to concentrate on what you really like to do and take it from there.

In terms of entertaining, being yourself means showing others what you love—your favorite things, and of course your favorite people. Call it atmosphere, ambiance, aura, but let it spring from your own preferences. Decide on your favorite atmosphere and set out to create it—whether romantic, streamlined, exotic, seductive, casual, festive, dramatic, nostalgic or avant-garde.

Once you've decided on the sort of atmosphere you'd like to create, tackle the technology of entertaining. Accomplished hosts and hostesses, like all good creative artists, first master the basic techniques of their craft. If they need to, they consult a decorator or take cooking lessons. If they feel comfortable without professional help, they let their own natural gifts flourish. They train themselves to be organized, and to plot party campaigns with the tactical ingenuity of a four-star general. The thoroughness and efficiency of their lists would shame a certified public accountant. Here in fact lies their most valuable skill: they acquire the art of planning ahead. Don't be afraid that careful planning will kill spontaneity: even improvised gatherings demand a certain amount of forethought to be cheerfully relaxed.

When starting to organize yourself, your surroundings, your plans for entertaining, set out to gratify all the senses by taking into consideration the sort of feeling, look, fragrances, tastes, and sounds you prefer and which, when properly pulled together, will make your hospitality memorable.

Let's start with the *feel* of successful entertaining, a quality at once tangible and elusive; ideally it should produce that exhilarating sensation called "having a wonderful time." Many factors contribute to a buoyant atmosphere, the principal one being an air of general comfort. Comfort itself has many component parts; possibly the most important one is a sense of order—as long as it doesn't get out of control and become too rigid. Strive for the happy medium, an aura of serene neatness, without becoming compulsive.

A welcome new trend is the use of decorative storage baskets and boxes of all shapes and sizes to keep everyday clutter under control. They come in everything from rough straw to gleaming acrylic, and are a godsend, particularly in small apartments. For frantic countdown clearing of the decks, just before your guests arrive, buy yourself a "horror basket" into which you can brazenly dump wet towels and bathmats (stashed in heavy-duty plastic bags), scattered articles of soiled clothing and other last-minute flotsam and jetsam.

One aspect of "counterfeit" you should avoid is the use of perfumed air fresheners. They don't really eliminate stale smells, only add a new element that may be equally bothersome. Throw open the windows; conceal *unscented* commercial deodorizing bottles behind furniture; shampoo the dog and inspect the cat.

Comfort also means a feeling of adequate space. Study your floor, seating, serving, table top, storage and traffic space. How can you expand it? If you can, turn kitchens, bedrooms or entrance halls into attractive dining and party areas. A remarkable range of furniture and equipment has been designed to help you—stack and folding chairs, over-sized floor and bed pillows, rolling carts and hot tables, collapsible and extension tables, modular storage units, vanishing stools . . .

Build in banquette seating. It is fashionable and relatively inexpensive to have constructed—or if you have a knack for carpentry, you can create one yourself. Another trend is to pull a dining table and extra chairs up to a bed, studio couch or love seat. The return of pedestals and plant stands has helped clear valuable floor and table space, just as the trusty old-fashioned drop leaf has come to the aid of harried cooks. You can never have too much table-top space at a party. When preparing to entertain, clear surfaces so that there is plenty of room to accommodate ashtrays, glasses, plates of hors d'oeuvres. While you're at it, move precious breakables out of harm's way. (If something does get broken, make light of it, even if you're ready to strangle the guilty party.)

Put on your traffic officer's helmet and take a look around. If you've invited a crowd, move furniture and small rugs to permit easy flow both around rooms and from one into another. Try to arrange your furniture so that guests can circulate without bumping their shins on low tables or having to ask others to move their chairs. Be flexible with seating arrangements; let people pull chairs together or shift floor cushions to form their own spontaneous knots. You can always discreetly slide them back to their original positions once the guests regroup. Be absolutely certain that you have seating space for each and every guest, unless you're giving the kind of large cocktail party or open house where you want to encourage your guests to circulate and entertain each other. For a really large party, it's best to push all movable furniture toward the walls. The result may remind you of a doctor's waiting room, but no one will notice once it begins to fill up. Remove any small tables which might get tipped over, and take up scatter rugs and animals skins unless they are skidproof.

Whether, like most of us, you're managing a party yourself or have called in outside help, make your guests feel at ease—without their noticing it. If you can't stay near the door yourself, have someone lurking within earshot of the bell to let people in, take their coats or direct them to a room where they can leave their things. People feel comforted by a mirror in the hall so that they can make swift repairs before the big entrance. If you've converted a bedroom into a coatroom, a collapsible clothes rack will minimize chaos when more than a dozen people are expected, unless, of course, you have ample closet space. Coatracks and hangers may be rented, but if you entertain more than once or twice a year in the colder months, it's uneconomical not to buy one or two and pop them together whenever needed. Hangers should be sturdy enough to hold heavy or damp coats without their collapsing into wrinkled bundles on the floor. Some people put out hairbrush, comb, clothesbrush, pin cushion, and travel-sized sewing kit on a dressing table or chest of drawers near a mirror, and a pad and pencils by the telephone. Do this kind of elaborate "laying out" only if you feel comfortable with it and not that you are "dressing up" in a way that's unnatural to you.

When your guests are ready to join the party, rescue them immediately from standing frightened at the door, in social limbo. At smaller parties, it's possible to introduce each new arrival to everyone else. But at large gatherings, when the numbers defeat you, steer newcomers to the most compatible group within reach and check from time to time to be sure that the conversation's taken off. (Incidentally, a great boon to hosts is the Continental custom of repeating one's own name when introduced, in case someone else hasn't caught it, or going a helpful step further, introducing oneself automatically. A simple "Good evening, my name is ——" is all that's called for.)

Sometimes, though people are more than their work, it helps to get a conversation going between two strangers to mention their profession, or perhaps a shared interest of another kind. Two skiers, for example, will spend hours comparing slopes together.

Comfort is feeling neither too hot nor too cold. It is amazing how quickly a large group of people can heat up a room. If you have such a thing, it's wise to turn the thermostat down to 60° or even a little lower, hours before guests arrive for a big party. Otherwise, turn off a radiator or two to cool the place down. There may be a slight chill in the air while you're still alone, but soon everyone will be warm enough. Keep bath or powder room, if not in the tropical, at least in the temperate zone.

Save open fires, no matter how they dress up the atmosphere, for smaller groups. At large gatherings a few martyrs inevitably get pinned next to the flames and suffer the torments of half-baking. On the other hand, if an unseasonable penetrating chill threatens to sabotage a convivial mood—a particularly glum situation in the country or at the beach—open fires and portable heaters can save the day, if there is not so much traffic that they cause a fire hazard.

Summer contributes its own set of problems. If you live in an apartment, without access to the great outdoors, don't plan to invite large groups during the hot months. This rule also holds for everyone hampered by inadequate terrace, porch or garden space. Oppressive heat can kill a party faster than a falling ceiling. If possible, start lowering the temperature days in advance. Keep shades drawn, air conditioners, if you have them, operating at full blast, and the kitchen door tightly shut. If you're not equipped with a kitchen exhaust fan, set a powerful portable fan in the window, facing outward, to expel heat quickly. Eliminate indoor candles and wait until the last minute to turn on a minimum of temperature-raising light bulbs. In any case, low lights lend a psychological aura of coolness.

And while we're on the subject of psychology, comfort, in the sense of social ease, means being able at all times to maintain poise. This applies to guest and host alike and explains the survival of good manners and certain useful codes of etiquette such as making proper introductions and avoiding antagonistic conversation. Making guests feel completely at ease is a host's most serious responsibility. While it's true that the pampered guest is the happy guest, beware of overkill. Seek out empty plates and glasses and enthusiastically propose refills. On the other hand, you needn't wheedle or make a tragicomedy about food going to beg, nor insist that someone accept an unwanted drink. And remember that pushing "a nightcap" on somebody who's clearly had enough can trigger disaster. Guests instinctively want to be guided, to know what is expected of them whether by a casual invitation to pour their own drinks or by a full briefing on an upcoming weekend so that appropriate clothes and sports gear can be packed. Try to anticipate confusion. Identify ashtrays, and if you want coasters to be used, then say so.

Don't gamble or play cards for money unless you are absolutely positive that each and every guest wants to do so and can afford to lose—even if it's only the cab fare home. If you're planning a meal where you think chopsticks are appropriate, provide forks and spoons for people who can't, or don't want to, use them. In the same vein of not asking too much of your guests, the timid or tongue-tied should not be obliged to make toasts.

When all is said and done, the vital factor in creating an exhilarating atmosphere is the guest list. The ideal party should both stimulate and soothe. Plan your guest lists with an eye to diversity of interests and talents as well as compatibility. Surprises in the form of unexpected or unusual people can ordinarily be counted on to generate a little extra excitement. At the same time, it's always a wise idea to include some cozy types, those wonderfully unaffected and amiable creatures whose sympathetic presence alone can convey more instant warmth and comfort than a roomful of swansdown pillows and security blankets.

The latest trends all point to great flexibility and imagination in mixing people, along with a growing refusal to "ask back" simply because you've been made to feel under obligation. Now, practically no one considers it a matter of life or death to invite even numbers. To everyone's relief, the tedious "boy-girl" syndrome is fast fading away, as are arbitrary age barriers which in recent years have made too many parties look like class reunions. It's both ridiculous and unfair to exclude a person you like from your list because you can't supply someone else of the opposite sex or of the same age. After all, you're not recreating Noah's Ark.

At one time or other you'll have to grapple with the "Can I bring a date?" dilemma. Grab it by the horns and respond frankly. If you've planned a seated dinner and don't want to expand or reshuffle or, more to the point, you actually haven't the space, explain that you're sorry but you can't fit any more in. Extend a sincere but unspecific "rain check" if the inquirer then begs off. However, it's always a kind and hospitable gesture to include out-of-towners, or visiting family and friends whenever possible, especially at larger parties when you aren't concerned about exact portions of food. As a matter of fact, it is just these unexpected guests who may supply that magical spark which turns a pleasant evening into a special event.

Today, most people invite their guests by picking up a telephone instead of a pen. With this method you know immediately who is coming and who is not, and you can juggle the guest list as you need to. For relatively formal occasions, you may want to follow up the phone invitation with a written reminder, especially since dinner plans are sometimes made two or three weeks in advance.

There are, of course, situations where you may want to use the traditional invitation our forebears thought was indispensable. For formal events which fall loosely into the "reception" category—weddings, dances—authentic engraving, if you can afford it, has a lovely feeling about it.

From the standpoint of saving time, written or printed invitations are the only solution for very large parties such as cocktails or open house. There are a wide variety of invitations of this sort. Choose according to your taste or whim, but try to avoid commercial cuteness. Many good-looking fill-in cards are now on the market, in bold or conservative colors and designs.

To give a large party an advance boost, let your imagination run free when choosing an invitation. Keep an eye out for amusing or beautiful postcards, for example, when traveling or on local jaunts to museums. If you have artistic ability, consult a reasonable printer and find out what can be done without too much expense, including photograph and picture reproductions.

the look

What are the visual aspects of entertaining that are creative and special? Once again, contemporary trends all seem to veer toward easy elegance and good quality made memorable by a host's individual stamp. Don't try to transform your home suddenly into your own version of Versailles. Enhance your natural surroundings, add a few touches that will make you, and your guests, feel festive.

First of all, study your lighting, the most crucial aspect of setting a mood and showing both your guests and surroundings at their best. The ideal degree of brightness is a question of personal taste; some hosts believe that blazing rooms keep party spirits at peak pitch, while others swear by the romantic glow of candles and the drama of cleverly concealed spotlights. To become your own lighting expert, play around with various equipment until you achieve optimum effects. Start with a couple of movable spotlights; today you can find them in every conceivable design—baby and pin spots, recessed floor and table models, standing lamps with swivel and adjustable parts.

You can add to your collection as you become more of a virtuoso. Invest in extra lengths of extension cord, double outlets, and a few pastel pink or pale amber light bulbs. Install dimmers if possible. Now go to work. Substituting pale pink bulbs for your usual clear ones can work miracles in changing a harsh clinical light to a flattering diffused glow. Such bulbs may not provide adequate strength for everyday needs, but the few minutes it takes to switch them before a party are more than worth the effort. Hide spotlights here and there, on the floor behind furniture, beamed on a work of art or an arrangement of flowers, plants or branches. The point is to experiment freely, taking pains, of course, not to electrocute yourself. Keep cords and attachments free from water and don't overload outlets. And while it is alleged that track-lighting is a lark to install by yourself, we'd recommend not only the advice and participation of an electrician but of a decorator as well. (An electrician can also save a lot of headaches when it comes to dramatic outdoor lighting.) Walk and sit everywhere that a guest might to be sure that no one will have an eye impaled by a naked shaft of light. If you're on the short side, ask somebody who is taller to go through the same performance, in case you've missed a blinding spot.

Candles somehow always seem to create a sense of the special, whether it's a single votive light set beside one perfect flower in a bud vase, or a room illuminated completely by blazing candelabra and sconces. Hurricane shades add a note of sparkling glamour, while at the same time protecting surfaces from draft-spattered wax and distracted guests from being set on fire. Candles can be color coordinated to your room and table décor, but most people seem to prefer subtle tones.

One of the delights of giving parties is that you can dress as you like, set the mood by what you, the host or hostess, are wearing. "Dress," Voltaire once pointed out, "changes the manners." When people dress in something other than everyday clothes, spirits lift, no matter how informal the event or casual the fashions. In today's style, this doesn't mean you must always wear evening clothes, but that you can wear something that you feel is fun or that makes you feel especially attractive, whatever its style. Don't run to the door with a fevered kitchen flush, hair and clothes awry from culinary exertions. Look gala, and your guests will follow your lead.

As to decorating with nature, floral designer James Goslee, for one private dinner, assembled superb centerpieces on black lacquer trays, mounding and mingling red roses and white iris, lemons, apples, oranges, limes, peaches, peppers, cabbages, leaves and wild grasses, fresia, gourds and wedges of watermelon.

While Mr. Goslee's lavish mélange is not a budget item, you also can get vivid variety without spending a fortune: combine single flowers of different species, each one in its own small vase or pot. A bud-vase garden makes just the right kind of welcome offbeat effect. Trend-setting florist Ronaldo Maia sets sprays of twigs on the table or potted plants on moss-carpeted soil, shells and sand, grasses and tall soaring rushes. He also uses all sorts of baskets which can be economically converted into tiny or giant vases simply by lowering watertight containers into them. Use anything—old-fashioned glasses, sand pails, wash tubs—as long as they fit snugly and won't tip over. His only restrictions are "never to wire flowers or force them into unnatural arrangements. You must give nature its head and let everything go naturally." This includes tulips, which tend to flop; to make them stand more at attention, drop a dozen pennies into their water. Other helpful tips include: beware of cut-rate flowers which have probably been overrefrigerated and will soon collapse. To do them justice, arrange flowers the evening before you entertain. Invest in plants rather than masses of cut leaves—you'll enjoy them much longer. After the party, change the flowers' water every day, clipping ¼ inch from the stems to prolong their life. Be sure that flowers and branches have room to breathe and plenty of water; don't strangle them in a narrow-mouthed vase. To help flowers hold their positions, squeeze crushed, tangled balls of chicken wire into their containers; the result will be a much more flexible and natural look than if you force them into a soggy styrofoam base which also cuts off adequate water absorption.

Mass together several flowering house plants for a dramatic jungle effect, or use them with fruit or vegetables and interesting objects to make lovely improvised still lifes. Be careful, though, not to crowd plants too close to candles or spotlights which can badly singe them.

Rob the kitchen to decorate the table, and once the party's over, consume the loot while it's still in good condition. Scout the markets or garden as if you were judging a beauty contest. Try not to limit yourself to the old-fashioned family fruit bowl, but search instead for the most varied and perfect candidates. Pile inky eggplants, garnet pomegranates, lavender plums, avocadoes, limes and clusters of black grapes up to the lower branches of a brightly laden pepper plant. Frilly blue-tinged Savoy cabbages can look positively fetching under candlelight on a bare wooden supper table. Or you can strew a runner of lemon leaves down the length of a formal dinner table, and nestle lady apples, speckled pears and knobby little cucumbers among the leaves, along with similar fruits and vegetables seen in Renaissance still lifes. Thrust a candle into the center of a magnificent bunch of asparagus which has been tied erect with a pastel ribbon. Lash bunches of grapes to the handle of a basket filled with field flowers and fruit. The trick is to fearlessly plunge ahead and experiment with whatever natural forms appeal most strongly to you.

Just as flowers have been liberated from funereal "set piece" bondage, so have table settings been freed. Today's best-dressed tables are decked out in "mix and match" fashions complemented by imaginative accessories. Collect party gear the way you buy clothes, keeping your eye open for all sorts of things appropriate to a variety of moods, hours and occasions. As Richard Knapple, Bloomingdale's trend-setting model-room designer, points out,"I believe you should have lots of things to use for table settings. Not just one set. Baskets, lacquerware, porcelain, stoneware. Tableprops, let's call them, so if you're doing an Oriental dinner, for example, you might do a setting like the one I've done for a small party (see color plate). An interesting setting like this contributes greatly to the ambiance and mood of the dinner. For a less formal effect, possibly for an Italian supper, you could use stoneware and heavy glass goblets instead. And I don't think one should just think in terms of entertaining people at a dining table. There should be several places to entertain—just to make it more interesting. Using the coffee table for an Oriental dinner is a good example."

Until quite recently anyone who gave dinner parties was expected to own at least one long damask, lace, cutwork or embroidered tablecloth with a dozen napkins to match. That you are now permitted to live without them will certainly come as a relief if you've paid a hand laundry lately. This is not to say that there is anything wrong with damask or lace cloths; if you already own some, use them as frequently as you can afford to.

All sorts of tablecloths, place mats and napkins are available today, and you can easily find something to harmonize with any mood or style. Mats come in every conceivable texture—mirror, vinyl, natural fibers, fragile laces, tough machine-washable fabrics—as well as in every conceivable color and pattern. Choose your favorite shape—rectangular, oval, round or square—and set off its color and texture with either contrasting or matching napkins, keeping in mind the china you'd like to team with them.

Mix and match cloths on the same table for a change. Richard Knapple says he prefers subtly colored table settings. Another decorator thinks that the best formula is to smooth a shorter cloth of a pale shade over a floor-length one of a more intense hue. In springtime, for example, he likes a short shell-pink cloth over a long lavender one complemented by bowls of lilacs and peonies. For a crisper look in summer, he throws a white cloth over a longer one in deep leaf green; daisies and white candles carry out the cool, night garden theme. For holiday buffet tables, try contrasting textures of red on red, with long full undercloths of flame velours topped by shorter ones of crimson linen.

Give yourself the freedom to mix china patterns at the same meal, too—as long as they look well together. Don't shy away from setting out your "best things" with the inexpensive. Price has nothing to do with visual appeal. Similarly, there is no longer reason to hide in shame if you haven't inherited or invested in the finest silverware. When planning a "wardrobe" of party equipment and accessories, budget not only in terms of money, but in terms of future hours you'll be obliged to spend on upkeep. Emily Post, in her etiquette book, informed her readers in 1922 that "In a small house, the butler polishes silver, but in a very big house one of the footmen is silver specialist, and does nothing else. Nothing!" The harrowing little picture she paints does much to explain the steadily increasing popularity of tarnish-proof flatware, serving dishes and table accessories. If you are, however, the proud possessor of beautiful silver, keep it gleaming (tarnish has a subtly nasty taste); when you're not using it, shine it up, shroud it tightly in plastic wrap, and keep it absolutely out of sight.

When choosing eating and serving implements, the one question to keep in mind is, Does each piece serve its intended function properly? Look for good balance and comfortable size as well as handsome lines and detail. Ask to try out flatware on a plate to be sure the pieces don't slide into the center or, worse, fall off the side too easily.

In the color plates you will find actual place settings. Bear in mind that new fashions in table setting include place cards even for informal meals, knife rests, miniature butter crocks, pepper and salt grinders, wine bottle coasters and carafes, manageably small plates for cocktail buffets and "tastings," and all sorts of decorative accessories and equipment.

As to serving dishes, as everyone knows, peasant or country dishes look appetizing and colorful in earthenware or iron casseroles brought straight from the stove. That's the way they were presented originally, and the way that suits them best. An extravagance such as caviar, on the other hand, is shown to best advantage when set like a jewel in a small crystal bowl nestled in crushed ice.

When first starting a collection of vessels to serve food in, it's best to focus on versatility and uncluttered design. Keep it simple when choosing basic necessities such as bowls and boards, baskets and pitchers, trays, platters, crocks and casseroles. Buy pieces you can use for more than one function; for example, a nest of white soufflé dishes can be used for all sorts of food; a good-looking chopping block can be used to serve cheese, bread, or raw vegetables or even a piece of broiled meat that will be sliced at the table. Concentrate on quality. It's much wiser to invest in one really good French chef's knife than two cheap knives, each designed to serve a single function.

Think about size in choosing a serving dish. You'll want enough space to frame the food appetizingly on the dish and to prevent spillage. A large straight-sided copper or enamel "stockpot," a broad round enameled iron paella pan with handles, and a long oval copper "gratin" pan are three invaluable cooking utensils which can also "come to table." Oversized bowls, platters and plates look sumptuous on buffet tables if you have the space, but they are awkward to pass at the table.

Food which has been shaped in a mold can always be counted on to create a gala mood. So can cake or pedestal plates and bowls which dramatically display food at different heights. Punch bowls, chafing dishes and wine buckets also spell instant festivity. Don't, though, limit yourself to what these things were traditionally intended for. Let your imagination run wild; for a wine cooler, you can use an enormous copper stew pan: at very large parties, try camouflaging commercial ice cube containers in anything from an umbrella stand to a mammoth terra cotta flower pot.

the presentation of drink

It used to be that only in Paris could you hear, for example, three plumbers on the Métro discussing the respective merits of how their wives cook duck and white turnips. Now, suddenly, in New York, in Duluth, in San Diego conversation about good food and drink is as popular as talk of politics and sports. As "gourmet cooking" and the enjoyment of wine have become more important in American life, patterns of entertaining have changed, and the focus of many parties has shifted from the bar to the table. Even ten years ago a host could count on an average of three to four drinks per guest before dinner. Today, the average number of pre-dinner drinks served is probably one or two, and many of your guests may ask for wine rather than spirits.

The built-in bar is fast becoming a period piece. Set out glasses, bottles, decanters and openers, stirrers and other paraphernalia any way you want—on a contemporary tea cart, in an antique armoire, on a skirted collapsible table, or on a dining room sideboard. You can convert a closet into a glamorous dispensary complete with mirrored walls, glass shelves, recessed lights and a mini-fridge. Or if you prefer, you can stash bottles in standing wine racks or even line them up in compartmental baskets on the floor beneath whatever constitutes your bar.

At many parties, there is a system close to self-service, with the hosts mixing the guests' first drinks and then urging them to help themselves to refills. Liberation notwithstanding, many women still feel inhibited about marching up to a bar to pour their own; if that is a problem among your friends, ask male guests to help in replenishing empty glasses. In either case, when guests are left to fend for themselves at the watering hole, make certain not only that all equipment and supplies have been laid in, but that they are easily identifiable, accessible and plentiful. You'll need appropriate glasses—highball, old fashioned and/or stemware, depending on the scope of drinks you offer. Two ice buckets speed self-service. A small wine cooler to hold one or two open bottles of chilled white wine won't take up too much space; keep reserved bottles either in a larger ice-filled container nearby on the floor or in the refrigerator. (Remember that once wine has been cooled it must not be allowed to return to room temperature—it physically cannot tolerate rechilling.) Again, depending on what you're serving, you'll need some or all of the following: a corkscrew, bottle opener, one or two long bar spoons, a water pitcher or carafe, small dishes (try using pale scallop shells) for strips of lemon and lime slices, olives, etc., soda, tonic, fruit juice or a grown-up soft drink such as bitter lemon, sugar syrup, a small sharp knife, a bar cloth or two, cocktail napkins, coasters, and bottles and decanters of spirits and apéritifs. There is a list on page 53 to guide you.

The particular drinks you serve, especially the type of whiskey, will depend on your guests' tastes, which may vary sharply, according to local customs. (A bar guide will be found on pages 54–55.) Most people don't bother any more with elaborate mixed drinks, and outside of a dry martini or a Bloody Mary, guests should gently but firmly be discouraged from requesting them. The exception, of course, is when you decide to concoct *one,* we repeat *one,* special potion such as a mint julep, milk or rum punch, black velvet, a whiskey sour or whatever you think most people will consider a treat. Still there will always be someone who'll react as if you were one of the Borgias, so have an innocuous alternative on hand; this applies also to champagne or white wine, which some personal chemistries find too acid. A really delicious holiday punch is an efficient way to serve a lot of guests swiftly, without having to go through the traffic-blocking process of rationing out fresh ice with each refill. This works particularly well when a punch bowl is set up on a round table around which guests can smoothly flow. And for non-drinkers, remember to provide something more festive than the ubiquitous ginger ale. Again, if you have space to set up a separate punch table for them, it will further facilitate serving.

service

The question of hired "help" depends a great deal on how much money you want to spend. Caterers claim that when expense is no object, the ideal ratio is one to ten. This means that if there are twenty guests, the caterer would recommend a bartender and one waiter or waitress passing hors d'oeuvres or helping at the buffet. Beyond this number, in Utopia, waiters or waitresses would be added accordingly. In the absence of servants, which for many people is the usual condition, everything depends on the energy of the host and hostess, their willingness to work, good planning, and the cooperation of good and trusted friends.

When plotting service and seating, it used to be necessary to think counterclockwise. The woman guest of honor (who would be considered so either because it was she for whom the party was being given, because of seniority, or because of official importance) was seated to the host's right, the male guest of honor to the hostess' right. Men would help to seat the women to their right. This system works as well as any other when there is someone actually being "honored." Otherwise seat people beside those they'll enjoy. Put on your right someone you want to talk to or who will need help in joining the fun.

Plates and food were traditionally presented to diners and removed from their left side, but only do that if it is convenient. There is nothing so silly as maneuvering a platter around a guest's head in a tight corner so as to serve from his left. Wine is served from the right, naturally enough, as the glasses are set out to the upper right of the plate. When an old "rule," like this one, is sensible, follow it. When it makes you uncomfortable or seems pretentious, forget it.

At a buffet, if you have a lot of guests, it's best to divide the service in two: lay out two stacks of plates, two sets of silver and napkins, two salad bowls, indeed, if possible, two sets of *everything* arranged in such a way that half the guests can be helping themselves from one side of the table while the others mirror their activities on the opposite side. Filled wine glasses should be presented from a second smaller table or sideboard. Dessert and coffee service depends on whether or not you have adequate help to clear away ravaged platters, bread crumbs, and other mess between the courses. If you haven't, steer clear of the main-course debris and serve the grand finales either from trays or from fresh tables or carts set up elsewhere.

the food

Suggestions for menus as well as recipes will appear later in the book. Interesting and feasible menu-planning is the key to good entertaining. If you don't have a flair for it, crib from parties you've enjoyed, study a few good books and magazine articles, concentrate on seasonal foods, which go well together and which are presented in an appealing way—without dabs of mayonnaise or drifts of paprika. Above all, don't experiment, either in menu or in new recipes on guests. Let your family and other nearest and dearest serve as guinea pigs.

Be as original as you like, but avoid gimmickry. Serve food that you honestly enjoy, rather than choosing dishes just because they're fashionable. This applies to all aspects of entertaining. Feeling compelled to entertain others in the same way they've entertained you is madness—why give a barbecue if it frustrates you to cook on a grill, or a cocktail bash if you can't stand crowds? Nor need you torpedo your bank account to "keep up" with others. Budget realistically. To treat friends to something special should be more of a challenge to your ingenuity than checkbook. A homemade peasant-style *pâté campagne* can taste as delicious as *foie gras* any day. On the other hand, if your incorrigible champagne tastes can be periodically gratified without undue strain, by all means alert your friends and get those corks popping.

One way to create a opulent impression without waste or fiscal worry is to offer a lavish amount of one or two simple and beautiful foods, such as a mammoth basket of autumn apples and a single huge wedge of cheese—the point being to introduce a giddy note of luxury rather than to show off. You can also give your hospitality an individual stamp by offering a "house special" whenever you entertain. This can be anything from an unusual blend of coffee to a homemade candy to a rare brand of liquor. One New York hostess' trademark is a glamorous cache of gold-tipped black Russian cigarettes. Bricktop, the legendary American expatriate entertainer and party giver, for years delighted chic French and Italian friends by invariably serving spareribs, black-eyed peas and sour mash bourbon. Whatever your culinary background, flaunt it rather than hide it if you know how to cook—whether it's Tex-Mex, Yankee or what one debonair New York host refers to as his "Western Pennsylvania ethnic" cuisine, which runs in a somewhat counterrevolutionary direction toward ham loafs, fresh peach pies and goblets of ice water. The same holds true for *haute cuisine* recipes which, once mastered, you now feel to be unworthy of your extraordinary talents. Your guests will welcome the superbly turned-out dish. Familiarity has probably bred contempt only as far as you are concerned.

Today, many people keep detailed party files, in which they record menus served to specific guests. This minimizes the chance of monotonous repetition in the future. But on holidays, or on special occasions such as anniversaries, don't be afraid of repeating yourself on an annual basis—launch your own traditions and your family and friends will grow to love them.

If the prospect of having to single-handedly turn out a complete party meal throws you into a fit of antisocial depression, do not despair. There are specialists other than expensive caterers to help you put the pieces together. Scour their shops for instant assistance, and you won't have to resort to packaged frozen dishes. A really good delicatessen can supply you with a first course of smoked fish or a shrimp salad to fill halved avocados as well as a cold main course of spit-roasted chicken or sliced meats and, for dessert, an international cheese board. Fish shops will often cook shrimp, crab and lobster for you, open oysters and clams, and sometimes pack cartons and jars of their own chowders, stews and cocktail sauces. Find a first-rate bakery that sells not only the usual run of pies, cakes and cookies, but other helpful fare such as quiches, puff-pastry hors d'oeuvres and offbeat breads which freeze well. Scan the service ads in local papers and magazines for additional help—you're more than likely to discover some enterprising soul who's preparing culinary specialties on a semiprofessional basis. If you find all this still beyond you, have a reputable Chinese or Mexican restauranteur deliver emergency aid in unmarked brown paper bags—transfer the food to your best serving dishes, and mum's the word.

organizing to entertain

Once you've decided what kind of party you'd like to give, the crucial element is to plan ahead with care. Make lists of everything you might possibly need and check them against your present stocks and supplies. Here is a suggested countdown of steps one can take to ensure a successful party:

1. Draw up guest list.
2. Set date.
3. Invite guests.
4. Plan menu (and appropriate décor if the menu suggests one).
5. Make detailed shopping lists.
6. Stock bar and wine rack.
7. Check party equipment, and order well in advance any items you need such as coat racks, extra chairs, glasses.
8. Check bathroom.
9. Order ice and flowers.
10. Shop for groceries and beverages.
11. Clean and polish.
12. Decorate, arrange flowers, set out candles, switch light bulbs, etc.

13. Set table, and get out necessary serving dishes and utensils.
14. Set bar, fill cigarette containers and candy jars, refuel lighters, put out matches and extra ashtrays.
15. Finish whatever chores you can in the kitchen.
16. Fill ice bucket.
17. Take a bath and a nap, and dress to greet your guests.

Having dutifully done all of this, you may still run into unforeseen emergencies. So try to forearm yourself with extra fuses, a reliable commercial spot remover, rock salt to melt ice slicks on steps or sidewalk, a fire extinguisher if you're using canned heat or alcohol burners, protective coverings between tablecloths and sensitive surfaces, a stand for dripping umbrellas, extra bar cloths for hasty mop-ups.

In conclusion we must warn you of another kind of emergency, one which, unfortunately, may be impossible to prevent: at some point one is liable to run afoul of the Odious Guest, a deadly species which includes, among others, the drunk and the deliberately rude. Hypocrisy is the best policy when dealing with someone who's had too much to drink, especially of the belligerent school. Verbal counterattacks are to be avoided at all costs, as they may lead to serious trouble. If possible, enlist unspoken aid; the most efficient technique to ease a drunk out the door is to get a self-sacrificing friend volunteer to see the casualty home, or at least into a cab. An Odious Guest doesn't necessarily have to overindulge to sabotage a party. If you have the bad luck to invite someone who thinks it's sophisticated to be insulting, keep your temper and afterward cross the offender out of your address book. Mercifully, such people are rare, for if there's one thing a well-planned party can achieve, it's to make each and every person notably rise to the occasion.

entertaining from morning to midnight

The inevitable first step when you decide to entertain recalls an ancient recipe for beef stew: "First you catch a cow." In other words, you've got to decide exactly what kind of party you're going to give before you can get started. Will it be at sun-up, high noon, dusk or dead of night? Will it be for two, twenty or two hundred? How much time, energy and money are you prepared to spend? To help you corral your cow, we've compiled a chronological list beginning with breakfasts and proceeding festively onward through the day and night. You'll find that each category has its own attractions and advantages; certainly at least one of them can be matched to your particular needs, mood and budget.

Many of the categories are fully discussed in the next chapter by hosts and hostesses who are known for giving certain kinds of parties especially well. Some prefer large cocktail bashes; others, quiet dinners. But whatever they prefer, their insights and tips should be of great help to anyone who feels inspired to follow their particular examples. The following rundown of parties is meant to trigger your imagination as to the many possible ways in which one can entertain. Whenever a category has not been fully discussed by at least one member of our panel of accomplished hosts and hostesses, we have supplemented their observations with suggested menus and brief lists of helpful party equipment. Selected recipes from these categories will appear on pages 173 through 208. For dishes not specifically described here, consult any really reliable general cookbook such as *James Beard's Menus for Entertaining*, *The Joy of Cooking* or *The New York Times Cookbook* by Craig Claiborne.

breakfasts and midmorning kaffeeklatsches

Excluding the elaborate "wedding breakfast" there are two basic types. The first is the short and sweet weekday meal, which permits you to catch a busy friend or two in midair or to review a civic or business project in a state of relative serenity. The second is the luxuriously lazy sort of meal where you can settle back and fritter away a weekend morning in the company of blissfully sedentary family and friends.

For the short and sweet variety, you have no time to waste dashing back and forth with relays of food and drink. Having everything prepared and at hand calls for wise menu planning. Juices and cut-up fruit are easy to serve and clear away. Baskets of napkin-wrapped hot breads stay warm and can be passed around by hand, as can decorative pots of jam and honey and crocks of butter. Once you are seated, the point is to stay put with as few interruptions as possible. Helpful equipment would include an electric coffee grinder, an electric coffee pot, a hot tray and a rolling tea cart. These menu suggestions may also be of assistance:

continental and other delicious simple breakfasts

An authentic "Continental breakfast" consists solely of brioches, croissants or crusty rolls slathered with sweet butter and a choice of honey and two jams, usually apricot and strawberry. Bitter espresso-style coffee and frothy hot milk are poured simultaneously from a pot and pitcher into a cup, mug or—if one really wants to escape into the Parisian past of Colette—a finger-toasting bowl. The proportions of milk, coffee and sugar vary according to taste. Most probably you will want to supplement this somewhat skimpy menu with juice or fruit, and a little protein such as soft-boiled eggs, delicate slices of ham, or for a northern European change of pace, a selection of imported mild yellow and bland cream cheeses.

In the spring or summer, you might offer an ethereal light breakfast of chilled fruit compote, composed of pink grapefruit and mango sections, drained leechees, honeydew and cantaloupe balls, preferably served in a fragile-hued Oriental bowl, accompanied by hot brioches or toasted English muffins, ginger marmalade and a pot of China tea. An updated, down-home warm-weather menu might include popovers or Bloomingdale's whole grain muffins (page 202), oven-crisped bacon, strawberries and cream, and tall glasses of iced coffee.

New York City's classic combination of toasted bagels, smoked salmon and Philadelphia cream cheese, possibly followed by a cold compote of stewed mixed dried fruits laced with rum or bourbon (the alcohol evaporates in the cooking) will effectively warm the cockles on a chilly morning when sturdier sustenance is welcomed. If you dare to be a true renegade, so will a steaming tureen of hearty soup, such as fresh vegetable and beef ladled over chunks of toasted French bread, or, a traditional New England fish chowder, which makes a wonderful creamy introduction to the day.

midday drinks

One of the main advantages of this kind of informal prelunch party is that you're not obliged to provide guests with a full meal. Here is the perfect occasion for concocting one, and only one, special drink for friends who, for all purposes, have been invited to drop by almost as if they were doing so spontaneously. Always serve some kind of appetizing "real" food (as opposed to processed) with drinks. Some suggested hors d'oeuvres to be served singly, or in a selection you like:

With a "Black Velvet" (page 204): oysters or clams on the half shell; crab claws or shrimp; miniature watercress and cucumber sandwiches.

With a Bloody Mary (page 203): any of the above; small *Croque monsieurs* (Gruyère and Virginia Ham sandwiches sautéed in butter and cut into squares); hot cheese puffs; crudités with Roquefort or sour cream and dill dip; blini, caviar or herring and sour cream.

With a Ramos Gin Fizz (page 204): toasted macadamia nuts; small smoked turkey and lime-sprinkled avocado sandwiches; shrimp tempura.

With sherry: Spanish *tapas* (page 43).

With Pernod or Greek ouzo: Eastern Mediterranean hors d'oeuvres such as stuffed vine leaves; cubes of salami and feta; flat Middle Eastern bread cut into triangles, toasted lightly, and dipped into creamily fluffy eggplant or chickpea and sesame pastes; red caviar with chopped scallion and tiny lemon segments on toast.

Good to own: large deep metal trays to pack with a bed of crushed ice for sea food; cocktail shaker; ice crusher.

brunch

"Brunch" usually means a leisurely and substantial breakfast sort of meal served some-where around lunchtime and enlivened with alcoholic drinks. Make it as casual or as lavish as you like, but keep it relaxed. As brunch is almost invariably served buffet style, it's best to dispense with knives and serve dishes which can be easily managed with a fork. Several good brunch dishes are stuffed crêpes (page 179); risotto with mushrooms (page 188); pasta shells in a sauce of cream, green peas, ham slivers, parsley and parmesan; finnan haddie; chicken, turkey, or corned beef hash; chicken livers sautéed with shallots, red wine and wild thyme; or classic standbys such as shirred eggs and sausages. A brunch is the time to serve baskets of hot breads, simple pass-around desserts like home-baked brownies and cookies which require no plates.

Good to own: Chafing dish; hot tray; gratin pan; covered casseroles or tureens; bread and cookie baskets; electric coffee pot or urn.

lunch

Lunch allows you to combine easy informality with more elaborate menus and table settings than accorded a brunch. Lunch is a good time to mix age groups at a small gathering; many older people prefer a lunch party to a dinner because of the difficulty of getting about at night. People also tend to drink less during the day than in the evening.

Lunch guests can be like newborn babies: once they arrive they tend to stay a very long time. Schedule accordingly. Unless you're all planning to move on to some kind of game or performance, don't ask people to arrive at high noon—you might even put them off until one-thirty or two. On the other hand, if you're planning to watch a televised game after lunch, invite them in time to get through the meal without rushing so that your living room won't be littered with dessert plates and coffee cups for the rest of the day.

With the exception of sturdy old-fashioned "Sunday lunches," menus should veer to the light and satisfying rather than the rich and soporific. However, if serving only two courses at table, provide something more than nuts in the way of hors d'oeuvres (see Brunches). Otherwise, it facilitates service to have a cold first course waiting at each place when guests seat themselves. Depending on the season, you might try:

A Warm Weather Lunch

Chilled soup: gazpacho (page 181), or pea and lettuce (page 180)

Cold poached chicken breasts, boned and skinned, masked in Dijon mustard and sour cream sauce and covered with halved seedless grapes

Rice Salad (page 182) with tomato wedges and Greek olives

Sultan's Garden (page 197), omitting grapes

Wine: Chablis, Pouilly Fuissé or Pinot Chardonnay

Iced Espresso

A Cold Weather Lunch

Salade Composée (page 182)
Steak and kidney pie in puff pastry
Pickled walnuts
Pear Sorbet (page 198): and Chocolate Meringue
    Cookies (page 200)
Wine: a good red burgundy
Espresso

For large numbers or outdoor gatherings, a buffet style lunch is almost obligatory. While you needn't try to recreate a cruise ship advertisement's culinary extravaganzas, a colorful variety of food makes a more exciting effect than one or two gargantuan offerings. Think smorgasbord, no matter what the ethnic origins of your menu. Reliable eye catchers are curries and brilliant arrays of condiments, piled into bowls, conch shells or scooped-out pineapple halves (cut straight down from the leafy crest through the stem end—the fruit can be cubed, tossed in kirsch and chilled for dessert). Or try a French charcuterie lunch with assorted dry sausages and salamis; pâtés; jambon persillé (ham cubes and masses of chopped parsley in a garlic-accented white wine, chicken broth and Madeira aspic); eggs mayonnaise; tomato, potato, baked beet and grated carrot salads tossed separately in seasoned olive oil and vinegar or lemon, and strewn with chopped herbs; salade niçoise (page 181); crusty bread—simply consult a comprehensive French cookbook and go to work.

At lunch you can use your prettiest china and linens in imaginative combinations to create ravishing flowerbed color effects. If you like, you can decorate the table with flowers and glassware and decorative objects, but forget the candles unless it's such a gloomy day that you decide to close the curtains and forget it all.

What drinks you serve is a matter of personal preference. Some people like Bloody Marys (page 203) or Screwdrivers, others prefer apéritifs such as Dubonnet, Lillet on the rocks with a twist of orange zest, Kir (page 206) with or without ice, Sangria or Vermouth. At a large lunch, you might offer nothing but the same wine you plan to serve with the meal—this way guests can keep the same glasses.

On extremely informal occasions where, for example, guests are contentedly lounging about in the sun, or glued to a TV sportscast, compose-your-own lunches are free-form and fun. Let guests construct their own sandwiches or salads from an attractive display of raw ingredients and dressings. In winter, one inventive hostess we know sets out stacks of

Richard Knapple

Mary Trainor Rice

Barbara D'Arcy

Richard Ryan

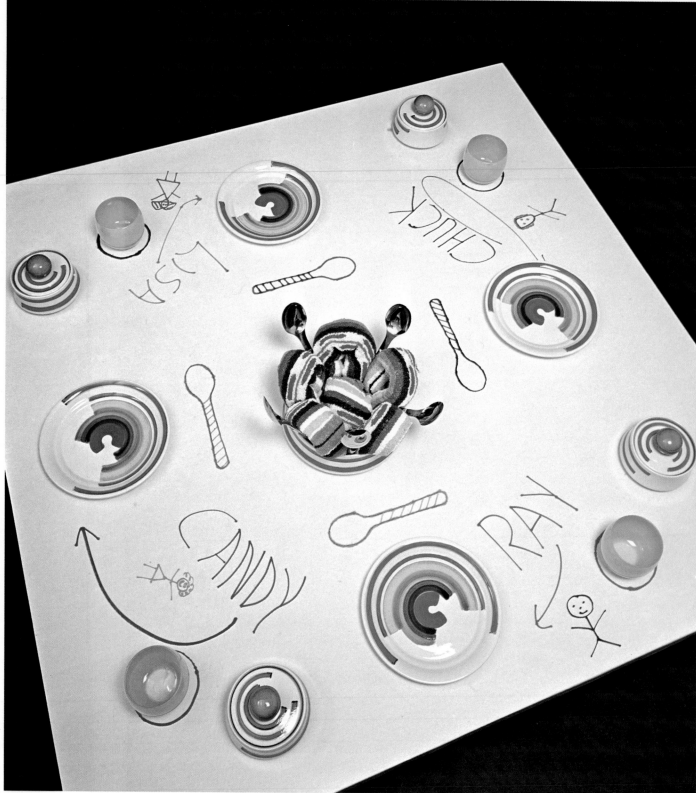

Candy Pratts

deep bowls and three tureens of different robust soups—a typical trio might be oyster stew, vegetable and onion—along with baskets of unusual breads, croutons, a cheese board and fruit. For drinks, you can continue the theme and set out a self-service bar, being sure to include something non-alcoholic such as minted iced tea or a spicy, freshly mixed Bloody Mary base. Beer, wine or sangria also go well with this sort of zesty do-it-yourself food.

picnics and barbecues

The greatest advantage of a picnic or barbecue, as far as the host is concerned, is that guests do not mess up the house. Picnics are the original movable feast; you can dispense picnic food almost anywhere—in the garden, on the slopes, at the beach or from the tailgate of a station wagon. A picnic or barbecue is an ideal solution to feeding slothful adults and restless children with a minimum of frayed nerves. When food is packed in individual portions, the young can be given theirs to eat when and how they like. By the same token, children can be appeased with a few quickly cooked hot dogs or hamburgers while more sophisticated adult fare is being unhurriedly attended to.

The secret of a really successful picnic or barbecue is thoughtful preparation and adequate equipment. Admittedly there is nothing you can do to control the weather, but in order to have on hand all the necessary food, drink, seasonings, utensils and other relevant paraphernalia, you must plan ahead.

It is important to keep picnic food and drink at optimum temperatures; this entails a variety of gear—thermos bottles and wide-mouthed jugs, insulated bags, containers of chemicals which can be frozen solid in the freezer, hibachis, spirit lamps, and styrofoam ice chests. Which of these you will need, and in what numbers, will naturally depend on the ambitiousness of your menu.

Today, service equipment for a picnic can run the gamut from paper plates and plastic forks to old-school Edwardian magnificence. James Beard uses his collection of huge double damask napkins only for picnics, and always brings along a basket of his best Baccarat wine glasses. Failing this, you might try to dress up your picnic with flat round woven rush plates to give added support to flimsy paper ones. Or buy individual wooden or enameled tin stack bowls which can be wiped clean between courses with a piece of bread or paper napkin. In addition you'll need gaily colored hot or cold paper or plastic-coated cups, bright paper napkins (and plenty of them) and good-looking contemporary flatware. Be sure to pack along a roll of paper towels, a cutting board and sharp knife, a corkscrew, salt shaker and pepper mill and plastic bags for refuse. When the earth or sand is damp, it's a comfort to own a cheap plastic tarpaulin, the kind used by house painters, to fold beneath blankets. Commercially packaged "towelettes," such as Wash 'n Dry, unglue sticky fingers when running water isn't available. And don't forget the insect repellent.

Picnic food may be as elaborate or simple as you choose. However, roast chicken, hard-boiled eggs, one or two raw vegetables, cheese, fresh fruit, bittersweet chocolate bars, wine and a thermos of espresso as a classic menu is hard to beat. Unless, of course, you take the suggestion of Anne Willan, director of Paris' La Varenne Cooking School and author of *Entertaining Menus,* and compose this "gourmet picnic for 10: Country terrine, salade niçoise (page 181), ratatouille (page 185), homebaked whole wheat bread, fresh peaches or pears, port salut or Gruyère cheese." Anne points out that this picnic "is portable as well as palatable, and all the dishes will survive without refrigeration for several hours." She also adds that both the terrines and salads are shown to best advantage in unadorned earthenware containers in which they have been cooked or prepared.

At a barbecue, everything depends on watchful timing; you cannot risk racing back and forth to the kitchen for an errant fork or spatula. Aside from the grill itself, you'll need plenty of asbestos potholders, long asbestos mitts, tongs, long-handled fork and spoon, basting brushes, foil, a narrow-necked water bottle to gently tame flames should they erupt too fiercely, and a fire extinguisher in case of unforeseen emergencies.

To break the hot dog and hamburger syndrome, you might try Luisa-Esther Flynn's Argentine mixed-grill barbecue (page 130) or Ruth Spear's butterflied leg of lamb (page 195), which cooks as quickly as a thick steak. This cut of lamb, which has recently become quite popular, adapts well to a variety of marinades, including a tantalizing Middle Eastern blend of fresh lemon juice, garlic, cumin and white pepper. Fish clamped in special holders and vegetables are also appearing more frequently over the coals or in the ashes, as the case may be. For a change of pace, try Carol Inouye's chicken yakitori (page 104), meatless shish kebabs, or thickish slices of eggplant or zucchini, cut lengthwise, painted generously with olive oil and broiled over low-burning coals. Corn and potatoes are also good wrapped in foil and baked slowly in hot ashes. Let people take their pick from a basket of vegetables and cook their own if they want to. However, for safety's sake, if there are too many children to supervise closely, don't let them toast their own hot dogs or marshmallows, no matter how shrill their outrage.

40

children's parties

These are tricky social events which usually demand tyrannical organization without overt bossiness, a very neat feat indeed. Children like visual surprises rather than edible ones, and games which are not overtaxing. They also like decorative themes—the circus, Snoopy, Mary Poppins, science fiction. (Ideally, *everything* should be disposable—plates, cups, tablecloths and decorations.) But most of all, and this will hardly come as a revelation, they like prizes and favors. If you want to establish a brilliant reputation with the pre-adolescent set, think in terms of loot, always remembering that it is quantity rather than quality that counts.

Confer with the birthday child about the menu—this way you'll learn what is acceptable within the peer group. If all of it sounds like plastic, make unalarming substitutions which almost any child will like—fresh orange juice or lemonade or a Forty Carrots milkshake (page 208) instead of ersatz tropical punch, strawberries dipped into frothily beaten egg white and super-fine sugar, carrot sticks, honey ice cream. Children are intrigued by miniaturization—make tiny biscuit "buns" to hold minuscular meat patties or silver-dollar-sized crêpes to smear with a favorite jam—it's fun to report that you've consumed seven hamburgers or thirteen pancakes at a single sitting. With regard to the number of guests themselves, let the guest of honor's personality guide you—gregarious children can cope with a riotous gang (ideally, out of doors), retiring ones are happiest with as few as two or three trusted friends. One final hint to the wise: there comes that point when children reach the Boisterous Period, and when the best party is *out of the house*. Take them to the circus, a bowling alley, a skating rink or anywhere else where hyperactivity will go unnoticed, and wait until they're teen-agers for the next party at home.

teas

The tea party would appear to be enjoying a rennaissance. As it can be either short or long in duration, can provide the solution to several social dilemmas—it is economical, one can fearlessly mix people who might otherwise not get along for a full-length evening party, and one can entertain teetotalers in a manner they'll truly enjoy. Also, a late tea is a particularly good way to entertain before a concert, play or movie when you don't want your attention fogged by firewater.

In the past, a traditional "English tea" featured small, thin, savory "tea sandwiches," some sort of hot buttered bread or muffin, jam and simple "tea cakes." On the other hand, a "high tea," such as Remi Saunder's classic Russian version (page 165), entails sufficient substantial food to be classified as a full meal. The first category might include a sampling of this:

Tea: Brew a blend of one part Earl Grey to three parts Darjeeling. Russian Caravan or Orange Pekoe make fine alternatives. If you're sufficiently ambitious to offer a choice, try a second teapot of smoky Lapsang Souchong, which is best sipped straight. Have a pot of hot water to dilute deliberately strong brews, paper-thin slices of seeded lemon, sugar and milk (not cream).

Sandwiches: Tea sandwiches take patience to prepare but are well worth the effort. Try a few of these at a time: Tongue with herbed green mayonnaise and capers. Shrimp butter, equal amounts of boiled shrimp and sweet butter pounded or blended to a paste with freshly ground white pepper and a squirt of lemon juice. Boneless sardines mashed smooth with horseradish, a squeeze of lemon and a few drops of heavy cream and tabasco. Peeled tomato slices with alfalfa sprouts and mustard mayonnaise. Hard-boiled egg rounds topped with sliced oil-packed artichoke hearts, pimento strips and mayonnaise. Virginia ham and sweet butter. Crab salad. Watercress or cucumber. Serve these on thinly sliced crustless breads of the best quality you can lay hands on.

As a hot tea bread, make scones, sugarless corn muffins, popovers, crustless cinnamon toast, or those faithful old stand-bys, toasted English muffins. Toast the bread and muffins in the oven so as to quickly and conveniently do many slices at once. Try to find an unusual jam such as plum-pear, strawberry-rhubarb or sour cherry to serve with buttered muffins or popovers.

For sweets, serve one rich cake such as mocha, maple or chocolate, and one plain one, possibly a nut loaf, glazed orange sponge or Bloomingdale's pound cake (page 202). You might also add or substitute a couple of pedestal dishes of small French and Viennese pastries.

The transition from tea to cocktails is an easy one. So, if people are staying on or coming in later for drinks, you can then bring out: Fresh sandwiches, which have been kept moist in a tight cocoon of plastic wrap, fresh salted almonds (page 178), a bowl of Greek olives, cherry tomatoes and raw vegetable strips (whichever vegetables you prefer—fennel makes a pleasant change), hot and sweet Italian sausages, sautéed with hot paprika or cumin, sliced on the bias and skewered with toothpicks.

To be properly equipped for a tea party, you'll need sufficient cups and saucers, small plates, cake (or fish or salad) forks, teaspoons, teapot(s), hot water pot or carafe, milk jug, sugar bowl, lemon dish, tea strainer. Two tables are a good idea if you have the space—one for the tea service, the other for food, plates and forks. Also nice to have is some kind of candle warmer or gentle spirit lamp to keep tea hot.

wine tastings

With the great interest many people are taking in wine today, a tasting becomes a viable alternative to the cocktail party. Aside from the wine itself, one needs only to have adequate table space and a supply of stemmed glasses. If both red and white wines are to be tasted, a minimum of two glasses should be allotted each guest. For tasting only one type of wine, a single glass will do. Food need be no more complicated than little cubes of cheese and thinly sliced bread. To learn how to stock a wine cellar and give wine tastings, study Peter Morell's helpful advice on pages 56 and 77.

sherry parties

Another effective way to break out of the standard cocktail party or midday drinks mold is to give a party where only sherry and "tapas"—simple Spanish hors d'oeuvres—are served. For a sherry party, you don't need to make the financial investment you do when stocking a bar for cocktails. While dry sherries, like white wine, should be served chilled, they should not be served on the rocks—this greatly facilitates self-service and automatically frees you from the ice-cube problem.

When accompanied by savory tapas, sherry should always be of the dry variety; a Fino or Amontillado, prechilled for 1 to 1½ hours in the refrigerator, is what's called for. Or, for a really bone-dry, tingling new taste, try a Manzanilla such as La Quita. True aficionados prefer to drink from pony-shaped, specifically designated "sherry glasses"; nevertheless, they will happily settle for any kind of white wine glass.

Some tapas are designed to be eaten from cocktail picks or with the fingers, others with forks from small plates either of the salad or bread-and-butter size. Salted almonds, Spanish olives, cubes of hard cheese such as cheddar, bite-sized slivers of prosciutto or cooked ham, pepperone sausage, slices of hot grilled pork tenderloin, wedges of cold potato omelet and chunks of bread. Plates will be needed for looser tapas—squid and potato salads, cold broiled and skinned red and green sweet pepper strips marinated in oil and vinegar, grilled or tinned sardines, or an authentic Spanish omelet, served in cold strips, made not with tomatoes but with sausage, potatoes and onion.

43

cocktail parties and variations thereupon

Cocktail parties, despite all protestations to the contrary, are alive and kicking. They are excellent vehicles for entertaining large mixed groups or for introducing a guest of honor to a wide circle of friends and acquaintances. Your major preoccupations will be: traffic flow, extra help and equipment, adequate supplies of liquor, ice and food. Clear the decks. Put out plenty of *big* ashtrays. Place any flower arrangements at or above eye level, otherwise they'll be wasted. Hire at least one bartender if you're expecting a mob (try a student employment office for reasonable fees) and set up another bar for self-service. If you haven't sufficient glasses (always count on guests' mislaying a maddening number and asking for replacements) rent them by the carton, or buy disposable plastic ones if they don't set your teeth on edge. One of the beauties of rented glasses is that they don't have to be washed—law usually demands that they be run through high-temperature sterilizers upon their return to the agency.

State laws also determine whether or not you can return unopened bottles of liquor to your dealer after a big party. If not, it might help to work out some sort of pooling system with friends who find themselves in the same predicament, a solution which can also prove useful when it comes to infrequently used equipment such as oversized ice buckets and punch bowls, chafing dishes, etc. If you can buy economical but ungainly large jugs of liquor, funnel them off into decanters or fifth or quart bottles, bearing the same label, of course. Buy mixes by the case, stacks of paper napkins, and order (or make in advance and store in plastic bags) more ice cubes than you think you'll need. Rather than bothering with fussy canapés, serve hors d'oeuvres that are distinctive, easy to pass and delicious to eat, such as Marinated Shrimp (page 177), Camembert Mousse (page 178), salted almonds (page 178), poached kielbasa (page 150) or piroshki (page 193).

cocktail buffets

At a cocktail buffet, you can invite as many people as you can comfortably hold. One of the beauties of the cocktail buffet is that guests feel they have been invited to a "real party," rather than merely being included in a body count and handed a drink. At a cocktail buffet, you can mix people wildly, crossing all age and interest barriers. This is the time to call all those people you've been meaning to get to know but somehow haven't done anything about.

Work out a traffic plan. Push furniture back from the center of the rooms and away from doorways. Especially if young people are to be included, reserve one room for music and dancing—you'll find that many older people may eventually join them. Be sure that guests can find fresh drinks without having to wait in a dispiriting line. Set up auxiliary self-service bars, even if it's only a card table with ice bucket, whiskey, wine, mixers, extra glasses and cocktail napkins.

Set up a buffet table or tables of food as far away from bar traffic as possible. The best arrangement is to have a long dining table in the center of the room so that guests can circulate about it. One should be able to eat cocktail-buffet food with fingers and wooden picks rather than forks; supply little bread-and-butter-sized china or handsome plastic-coated paper plates, though, to help keep food from spilling on clothes and carpets.

For a large cocktail buffet, you'll need at least one bartender and also kitchen help to retrieve dirty plates, glasses and ashtrays, tidy up and replenish food and possibly perform other chores, such as hanging coats on collapsible racks and carving. Or, you could follow Marina and Guy de Brantes' sterling example and train the younger generation to take over (page 86).

Especially if you've invited a mob scene, you might try serving a festive dry punch (page 207) along with the usual drinks. Set up a separate table out of harm's (and the bar's) way, drape it *almost* to the floor and center it with a large punch bowl, its base festooned with greenery or flowers, along with a ladle, punch cups and an extravagant stack of pretty paper napkins. If you don't want to bother with cups, use old-fashioned or stemmed glasses.

As mentioned previously, one should be able to eat cocktail-buffet food from little plates with the fingers or cocktail picks. This means that all meats must be carved into manageable pieces. For guests to make their own sandwiches, prepare a lot of halved and buttered slices of bread. Trim the crusts from all but "party rye" or French breads; small hot biscuits are good with baked ham, and miniature buttered rolls, split not quite in two, are excellent with nondrip seafood salads or solid mousses, which can be spread like soft pâtés. If you can lay your hands on a big chafing dish or two, serve tiny new potatoes to dunk in red caviar, sour cream and chives; herbed meatballs in caper sauce; bay scallops sautéed briefly and smothered in chopped parsley and tarragon; or miniature gefilte fish balls heated gently with hot curry powder and lime juice. Cheese boards and platters of raw vegetables are both decorative and delicious; however, banish "instant dips" and experiment with unusual dunking sauces such as an Italian "bagna cauda" (page 179). Crisply cooked vegetables marinated à *la Grèque* or in a herbed vinaigrette sauce are also colorful and provide a welcome change of texture.

Equip yourself with capacious ice containers, collapsible tables and coat racks, punch bowl and cups, chafing dish or spirit lamp, small plates, large platters, serving dishes, baskets and boards, extra ashtrays and, if you like, disposable plastic glasses. With an eye to foul weather and other emergencies, you might devise some kind of large umbrella stand, and lay in a reserve of plastic sheeting to slip beneath tablecloths or spread on the floor in a narrow strip to receive grubby galoshes and boots.

seated dinners

That the seated dinner is probably the most enthusiastically practiced form of entertaining today may be explained by its irresistible charms—specifically the simultaneous enjoyment of companionship, sparkling conversation and tantalizing food and drink.

The trick to giving a successful dinner party is to make the evening flow smoothly from start to finish. To achieve this, you'll have to try to steer clear of as many interruptions as possible. Unlike a minuet or a forced march, a dinner party should proceed naturally at its own spontaneous tempo. The only time you should turn into a cruise director is when you want guests to take their places for a nimbly timed meal. Place cards facilitate these maneuvers. If you wisely decide to separate people who've been glued to each other too long before dinner, have a master seating plan drawn up so that you won't have to lurch around the table like Chicken Little trying, at the last moment, to reshuffle names.

Round tables are particularly conducive to uninterrupted group conversation, as many wise hosts have discovered in recent years. Unless you're giving a really small dinner for four or five, don't plan to carve at table—the lull can become infectious. And if the conversations' crackling along, serve coffee right where you are.

If you're giving a dinner party single-handedly, work out the most fluid and inconspicuous service plan possible. Hot trays are a boon; you can set up the main course on a sideboard or table and have guests serve themselves while you clear away the first course. Rolling carts are also a great help, particularly those with more than two shelf surfaces. If, for example, you plan to serve a main course followed in turn by salad/cheese and a dessert, you could employ these tactics: 1) Leave the bottommost shelf free to stack dirty dinner plates; 2) This done, remove clean salad plates, cheese board, bread basket and salad bowl from second shelf and pass them; 3) When finished with these, return everything, including used forks, knives and plates to second shelf; 4) From top shelf take dessert plates and dessert and either serve everyone yourself or pass both around the table. If you have the space, you may even have after-dinner coffee cups, spoons, cream and sugar ready to pass, so that all you have to do after retrieving the dessert plates is to trundle the cart into the kitchen and return with a pot of hot coffee.

In recent years, the trends in food at dinner parties have reflected the overall social shift to a general paring down without loss of elegance. Three courses are the norm, with the first one often served in the living room with drinks—smoked salmon, marinated shrimp, pâté ... or, in cold weather, a cup of steaming bouillon laced with Madeira.

Increasingly, glorious vegetable dishes are vying with meats for the starring role of a main course. Taking a tip from the French, many people have begun to serve a beautifully prepared and presented vegetable as a separate course, either before or after the main one. Chinese quick stir-fry cooking techniques keep you in the kitchen for only a few minutes before calling guests to the table. If everything's sliced, chopped and otherwise ready to go, a deftly tossed stir-fry of snow peas, scallions, mushrooms, celery, water chestnuts, seasoned with a little garlic, fresh ginger and soy and the last-moment addition of a large bunch of watercress leaves makes an unexpected and delectable overture to a meal. Buy a wok and begin to experiment.

Food processors and powerful blenders also open up delicious new horizons; coarse or smooth fresh vegetable purées *au naturel,* sparked with either heavy cream, a little meat juice, nutmeg or fresh herbs are elegant accompaniments to simple meat, poultry and fish dishes.

Rich main courses are increasingly followed by light, calorie-conscious desserts, such as sorbets—revitalizing fresh fruit sherbets which you can make in the freezing compartment or an electric ice cream machine. Experiment with unusual flavors, such as pear (page 198), rhubarb sweetened with currant jelly, fresh minted lime, pineapple-rum, strawberry-honey-lemon or gingered melon.

buffet dinner parties

Buffet dinner parties solve the dilemma of entertaining when dining table space is limited or nonexistent. This kind of party is good for mixing guests who may not have enough in common to spend a full evening seated next to each other. Self-service allows people to regroup without seeming rude and also lightens the work load on the hosts and/or whatever help they may have brought in for the party.

You can give buffet dinners for as many people as you, your house and your party equipment can accommodate. There should be someplace, even if only a staircase or floor cushion for everyone to sit. Large serving vessels are preferable to small ones which constantly have to be refilled. Chafing dishes and warmers keep food hot between first and second helpings. It's wise to set up a separate table for wine and glasses, and if you have no sideboard and space permits, another for plates, napkins and silverware. Be sure to work out an efficient way to clear plates into the kitchen as soon as they've been relinquished; the deserted battlefield look created by abandoned dirty dishes casts a decided pall over a festive atmosphere.

For limited numbers, individual collapsible tray-tables mean your guests don't have to balance plates and cutlery on their laps. For larger numbers, menus which do not require knives work best. A variety of food makes a gala effect, but beware of potentially messy dishes such as spaghetti or floppy-leafed green salads which can spatter clothes, floors and furniture. People tend to take smaller portions at a large buffet than they would at a seated dinner, perhaps out of consideration for others yet to serve themselves. So don't be alarmed if a lot of food remains after the first go-around—buffet guests can usually be counted on to return for seconds. Magnums of wine look festive and facilitate service at a large buffet. Serving homemade candies instead of dessert eliminates repeated traffic turmoil, not to mention a second avalanche of dirty dishes (see recipes for apricot sugarplums, page 203, and sherried walnuts, page 202). Some hosts have further simplified their lives by not offering coffee unless guests specifically request it, but this may not suit your particular guests.

after-the-theater and other late suppers

An after-theater supper has one advantage in particular to commend it: no matter how good or bad the performance may have been, everyone in the group is on common conversational ground—an excellent way to make a party self-ignite. For large late suppers, see page 47. For cozier ones, we'd suggest no more guests than you can comfortably seat at one table. Have everything meticulously organized and prepared in advance, including a filled ice-bucket, chilled wine, and food calling for a minimum of last-minute manipulation. Base your menu on dishes which can withstand a brisk reheating or which are best served tepid or cold. While late supper fare should be satisfyingly substantial, it should not induce a sleepless night. Nor should it be overly bland—a direct zing to the taste buds is what you want as the witching hour looms. The Italians have the right idea with their late night risottos and no-nonsense pastas. Accordingly here is one supper menu featuring

Saffron Risotto with Cognac-Flamed Mushrooms
   (page 188)
Mixed Green Salad with Lemon and Oil Dressing
Toasted Triangles of Middle Eastern Bread
Worldly Sundaes (page 201)

Or you might try this cold alternative:

Salade Composée with Baked Beets (page 182)
Platter of Smoked Meats
Spiced Crab Apples and Watermelon Pickle
Hot Crusty Bread with Sweet Butter
Worldly Sundaes

No matter how they protest to the contrary, most people love desserts. An easy and amusing one to serve at a late supper is the Worldly Sundae. Simply fill a gleaming glass or crystal bowl with scoops of different flavored ice cream and send it around the table with a selection of heady liqueurs. This is also a canny way of solving the problem of after-dinner drinks—they're in the dessert. As a decorative touch, decant the liqueurs into a collection of antique perfume bottles or small stoppered contemporary flasks. You needn't label them—sniffing is part of the fun.

after-dinner gatherings and entertainments

Informality is the keynote to these relatively undemanding social occasions when friends drop by for a drink, coffee and dessert, a game of cards, or simply to chat and listen to records. Here is a good time to bring out a special treat such as Irish Coffee (page 206) or the Four Seasons' deliciously surrealistic Coffee Cup Soufflé (page 199). Or borrow from the Greeks who, when dancing or listening to music late into the night, voluptuously stoke themselves with floods of wine and platters of fresh fruit cut into chunks and speared with wooden picks. For a somewhat sturdier snack, you might reproduce one of Bloomingdale's "Ondine" Danish open-face sandwiches: either crabmeat and celery salad or rare roast beef with sliced egg and horseradish sauce on sour rye, or trimmed slices of meal bread slathered with Danish camembert and topped with tomato rounds and strips of crisp bacon. Serve these with glasses of icy beer or wine. But whatever you decide to serve, relax and enjoy the evening—and so will your friends.

equipment and supplies

stocking the bar

Alfred Winograd, proprietor of Madison Avenue's Gourmet Liquor Shop, has for years advised everyone from neophyte party-givers to New York's most experienced hosts on keeping a well-stocked bar. Mr. Winograd has made the following selections with different budgets in mind:

a well-equipped bar

Basics

Minimum of 6 to 12 all-purpose stemmed wine glasses
Minimum of 6 to 12 highball glasses
Corkscrew
Bottle opener
Ice-bucket and tongs
2-ounce jigger
2 carafes or pitchers for water, Bloody Marys, jug wine, etc.
Bar cloth
Cocktail napkins
Small dishes for lemon peel, etc.
Bar spoon
Bar knife zester

Nice to Have and No Budget

Old-fashioned glasses, regular and/or double sized
Brandy snifters
Outsized wine glasses
Pony glasses
Pilsner glasses
Liqueur glasses
Muddler
Wine cooler
Cocktail shaker with strainer
Decanters
Sugar syrup bottle
Silver mint-julep mugs
Bar tray
Large auxiliary ice-bucket
Compartmental baskets for extra bottles of spirits, wine and mixers

Modest Budget	Nice to Have	No Budget
5 to 8 bottles	10 to 12 bottles	14 to 24 bottles
Apéritifs (Choice of 2)	**Apéritifs** (Choice of 3)	**Apéritifs** (Choice of 4 to 6)
1 dry vermouth—American 1 sweet vermouth 1 dry sherry	1 dry vermouth 1 sweet vermouth 1 quinine-based apéritif (e.g., Dubonnet, Lillet, Byrrh)	1 dry vermouth 1 sweet vermouth 1 dry sherry 1 cream sherry 2 specialty apéritifs (e.g., Campari, Dubonnet, Punt-e-mes, Cynar) 1 Pernod or Ricard
Liquors (Choice of 2 to 4)	**Liquors** (Choice of 4 to 6)	**Liquors** (Choice of 6 to 8)
1 blended whiskey 1 Scotch whiskey 1 vodka—80 proof 1 gin	1 Scotch whiskey 1 bourbon whiskey 1 Canadian whiskey 1 gin 1 vodka 1 rum 1 blended whiskey	2 Scotch whiskies (1 unblended and 1 premium blended) 2 bourbon whiskies (1 premium and 1 good) 2 Canadian whiskies (1 premium and 1 good) 1 gin—imported 1 rum 2 vodka—1 imported and 1 domestic

Modest Budget	Nice to Have	No Budget
5 to 8 bottles	10 to 12 bottles	14 to 24 bottles
Cordials & Brandies (Choice of 1 to 2)	**Cordials & Brandies** (Choice of 3)	**Cordials & Brandies** (Choice of 4 to 10)
1 brandy 1 crème de menthe	1 fruit-flavored liqueur or brandy 1 crème de menthe or cacao 1 brandy	1 fruit liqueur 1 crème de menthe 3 specialty items (e.g., Drambuie, Galliano, Strega, Benedictine, Chartreuse, Grand Marnier, Cointreau) 2 brandies (1 cognac and 1 armagnac or other) 1 eau de vie (e.g., kirsch, framboise, pear brandy) 1 coffee, chocolate or crème de cacao 1 anise liqueur (e.g., Sambuca, anisette)

peter morrell's ideal 48-bottle wine cellar

Red

Beaujolais:
Brouilly (3)

Rhône:
Côtes du Rhône (2)

Burgundy:
Côtes de Beaune (2)
Côtes de Nuits (2)

Bordeaux:
Médoc (2)
St.-Émilion (2)
Graves (1) }
Pomerol (1) } château wines

California:
a good Zinfandel (1)
a good Cabernet (1)
Petite Syrah (1)
Pinot Noir (1)

Italian:
Spanna (1)
Bardolino (1)

White

Everyday:
Blanc de Blanc (3)

Burgundy:
Chassagne-Montrachet
   Blanc (1)
Chablis (1)
Meursault (1)

Mâconais:
Mâcon Blanc (2)

Italian:
Pinot Grigio (1)
Verdicchio (1)
Corvo (Sicily) (1)

German:
a good Rhine
   Johannisberger (1)
a good Moselle
   Piesporter (1)

Alsace:
Gewürztraminer (1)
Sylvaner (1)

Loire:
Pouilly-Fuissé (1)
Sancerre (1)
Vouvray (1)

Rosé

Tavel Rosé (1)
Provence Rosé (1)

Sparkling

Loire:
Dry White Sparkling Loire (1)

Champagne from France:
2 half bottles (*not* splits)

Champagne Korbell (1)

Port

Porto (1)

party gear

electrical equipment

Basics

Blender
Mixer
Electric coffee maker

Nice to Have

Oven toaster
Deep-fat fryer
Electric skillet
Meat grinder
Coffee grinder

Nice to Have, cont.

Ice-cream maker
Hot tray
Dishwasher

No Budget

Food processor
Mixer with accessories
Ice maker
Hot table
Espresso machine
Ice crusher

equipment for the table

Basics

Linen: 6 place mats of machine-washable
    fabric, straw or plastic
6 napkins of machine-washable fabric

Nice to Have

Solid or print tablecloths
Contrasting or matching napkins
Heatproof place-mat pads

Nice to Have, cont.

Linen or fine fabric place-mats
Vinyl or mirror place-mats

No Budget

Embroidered linens
Lace or organdy appliqué cloths
Accessorized napkins
Lacy colored linen cloths

china

Basics

White ironstone service for 8, including 8 dinner plates, 8 cups and saucers, 8 salad bread-and-butter dishes, one round serving bowl, 2 platters.

Nice to Have

Earthenware or china service for 12, including dinner plates, salad bowls, bread-and-butter plates, cups and saucers, soup bowls, fruit plates, 1 14-inch platter, 1 16-inch platter, 2 oval vegetable serving dishes.

No Budget

5-piece china service for 24, and in addition:
24 cream soups and saucers
24 demitasse cups and saucers (mixed or matched)
2 16-inch platters
1 outsized platter (for turkey, poached fish, etc.)
3 large round serving bowls
24 fruit saucers
1 gravy bowl
24 artichoke plates
Large covered tureen
24 covered pot au crèmes
Cake and pedestal dishes

flatware

Basics

Stainless flatware or uncluttered design, service for 8

Nice to Have

Silver plate, 5-piece settings, service for 12, and in addition:
12 teaspoons
12 butter spreaders
2 serving spoons

No Budget

Sterling silver 6-piece setting, service for 24, and in addition:
1 sterling tea and coffee service with tray
12 additional spoons
24 cocktail forks
24 fruit knives and forks
24 cream soups
24 fish forks
24 fish knives
24 stemmed sherbets

(flatware, cont.)

Nice to Have

flatware, cont.

Nice to Have

2 serving forks
1 cold meat fork
1 cake server
1 gravy ladle
1 sugar spoon
1 soup ladle
1 carving knife and fork
1 salad serving spoon and fork

No Budget

3 cold meat forks
2 gravy ladles
1 soup ladle
4 tablespoons
2 salad serving forks
2 salad serving spoons
1 carving fork and knife
1 long-handled stuffing spoon
1 cake server
1 cheese server

glassware

Basics

8 goblets, eight 8-ounce wines, 8 old-
fashioned glasses

Nice to Have

12 goblets, 12 wines, 12 champagnes, 12
cordials, 12 highballs, 12 double old-
fashioneds, 12 snifters, 12 pilsners, 12
finger bowls

No Budget

24 ballon wine glasses
24 tulip wine glasses
24 champagne glasses
24 snifters

24 cordials
24 highballs
24 old-fashioneds
24 crystal salad or service plates

No Budget

table accessories

Basics

Salad bowl, pitcher, wine flask, 2 to 4 candleholders or candlesticks, coffee and/or tea pot, ashtrays

The amount one spends on additional table accessories depends on the materials from which they are made, as well as the quantity in which you buy them; sterling silver candelabra, for example, obviously represent a greater financial investment than pewter or glass. Keeping this in mind, the following might be added to your repertory of party equipment: pitchers, decanters, wine or champagne coolers, lidded or plain serving dishes, tureens, relish dishes, fruit and flower bowls, regular-sized and bud vases, candlesticks and candelabra, ashtrays, cigarette containers and matchboxes. Purely decorative objects, as a matter of personal taste, can take any form that captures your imagination.

creative hosts

james beard

James Beard, reigning guru of American cuisine, dean of culinary educators, irrepressible bon vivant, is also a justifiably celebrated host. Among his many best-selling books on gastronomy are the contemporary classics *American Cookery*, *Beard on Bread* and *Menus for Entertaining*.

preferences

Lunches for 6 or 8: "My favorite meal, and not only on weekends. So few people give them any more, and it's such a shame. A lunch during the middle of the week, as long as you don't keep people too long from their daily obligations, is a delightful break from the usual routine."

Dinners for 8 or 10: "With limited numbers you can give better food."

Buffets for 14 and up: "Three, or on occasion even four, courses of cold food with one hot dish. Numbers all depend on what you've got in the way of chairs."

Large cocktail parties: "With a limited choice of two or three drinks and a big buffet, every once in a while I love to do a bash. You should always invite more than you can accommodate. You have to go to extremes. I like to get hordes of people crawling around and beating against each other. Pile them up to the rafters, then settle back and watch."

Kitchen parties and picnics: "Because I don't like staid forms of entertaining."

The secret of entertaining, Jim feels, is a combination of exciting food and show-manship. One can turn to his many books to produce the first, but how does one acquire the second? A former opera singer, he muses a moment, then murmurs wickedly, "You have to spend three years in the theater, I guess. Quite seriously, though, entertaining amounts to a theatrical production. You're not only the producer and director, but what with coordinating the grocer, the butcher, the florist, et cetera, you become the stage manager and the set designer as well. Above all, a great deal has to do with personality. There are two entirely different kinds of hosts—those who themselves are the center of attraction, or those who express themselves with food, flowers and such and then slip quietly into the background. I'm definitely one of the latter. You pull people together, get it going, then you're the puppeteer."

Whatever the subject under discussion, Mr. Beard is never reticent about his likes and dislikes. Prominent among his social peeves are hosts who keep their guests drinking too long before a meal. The appropriate time to allot for drinks, he feels, is thirty to forty minutes before dinner, fifteen to twenty minutes before lunch. "The whole charm of a lunch or dinner is conversation at table, not beforehand." Timing of meals is very important, so if you've planned ahead properly, a cocktail hour of thirty to forty-five minutes is ample and easier on the cook and guests than a longer one. Once you're seated you can stay put as long as you like. I would always rather linger at the table—of course, I'm a rebel. Rather than interrupt conversation, I'll serve the coffee right there."

Occasionally, Jim emulates one Cincinnati hostess whose guests are handed a card when they enter saying, "You will be sitting next to — and —," fair warning not to monopolize these individuals over drinks. He prefers not to interrupt conversations to make introductions. In fact, on this point he is outspoken: "I think too many people are introduced to too many other people anyway. If people have any social sense at all, they'll get themselves into a group. However, he does introduce guests to the dinner menu, written out in the French manner on a porcelain menu card which is conspicuously placed either on the dining table or possibly in the drawing room before dinner. This way they will not make the blunder of taking too many helpings of a first course when a copious second one is on its way.

As a growing trend, entertaining in the kitchen receives Jim's unqualified endorsement. A friend in California has just finished building a marvelous house where the kitchen, dining and drawing room are all in one," a perfect atmosphere, Jim feels, for a formal dinner—"I like the idea of switching back and forth from an apron to a dinner jacket. As nobody has servants any longer, more people should design houses this way."

atmosphere

Mr. Beard's conviction that all the world's a stage, at least as far as entertaining is concerned, is strikingly illustrated by the décor of his Greenwich Village town house. Guests usually first convene on the parlor floor in a room dominated by Chinese and European sculpture, mirrored screens, yellow-cushioned antiques and embroidered mandarin robes. One almost expects to find the host sitting by the fireside, sipping champagne and solving terrible murders. The ground floor is given over entirely to the production and consumption of superb food and drink. The dining room, papered in a dramatic black-and-white vine leaf pattern and hung with food still lifes, is intriguingly eclectic. A round marble table dominates the center, and a small semicircular console—in a pinch it can accommodate three or four surplus diners—is pushed beneath windows in which Russian hurricane lamps flicker. This room leads directly into a large and functional butter-yellow kitchen, as intricately designed as a Chinese puzzle. Beyond this copper-strewn alchemist's workshop lies a garden jammed with statuary, bushy pots of herbs and a splashing fountain.

To entertain well, a host or hostess ideally should be equipped with "loads of glasses and silverware and dishes, dishes, dishes." However, there is no need to own enormous sets of china, with everything matching from the first course through the dessert; Mr. Beard likes to mix different sets of patterns at the same meal. His favorite glass is a Baccarat modified *"ballon"* ("Bourgogne" or "Trianon"), which he uses for all wines. He also collects unusual and capacious containers—huge vases, wooden buckets, punch bowls—that can double as wine coolers. Aspiring hosts are warned, "If you intend to cook for big groups of people, you must have the equipment to accommodate large quantities of food. Enormous pots are what you need—a twelve- or fifteen-quart stockpot is wonderful. A hot cupboard for keeping food and plates warm is also nice to have. A Cuisinart food processor can be a savior. And you *must* have a collection of good sharp knives—you should keep them that way with a small sharpener like a Zip-Zap, which I've come to the conclusion is best."

food and drink

A seated dinner chez Beard, as one might imagine, can be an unforgettable excursion into the stratosphere of *haute cuisine*. Even at its most rarefied, however, the menu will never be overly elaborate. Jim casts his ballot for simplicity. "Too many people think you have to have hot meats. They don't understand that many things—baked ham, roast beef, roast or fried chicken—are best served tepid." He also points out that one really good salad is far superior to a variety of undistinguished ones. What could be better, he asks, than a seafood salad followed by a crisp roast chicken, just barely warmed through, a hot vegetable, and then everything topped off with some sort of delicious fruit dessert and cookies? "If I have a great deal of wine, then I'll serve cheese, which makes a fourth course. At a buffet, for God's sake, be sure to guide your guests so they won't put everything piled on the same plate."

Jim, who likes to serve champagne before dinner, notices that more and more people "even two-fisted drinkers" are asking for white wine, with or without a dash of cassis, at cocktail time, perhaps out of an awareness that more wine is to come. Almost no one, he says, stocks a limitless bar any longer. As for service, he recommends that the host or a close friend tend to the drinks—"Don't have guests make their own. They become sloppy and inclined to pour too much, especially spirits. You have to be very keen on how many drinks people are going to have if you want to be proud of your dinner."

And what of those "bashes," those huge cocktail parties where guests are "piled to the rafters"? Explosions of laughter as Mr. Beard cautions the intrepid hosts that "They'll have to risk getting their clothes out of press—or completely torn off!" When feeding the drinking masses, Jim disdains platters of "little doots and dots, which I fervently hope are gone, gone forever. Hooray! They're a pain to anyone who makes them and a pain to eat. Nor do I go along with this general passion for crudités. You spend hours cutting up all those raw vegetables. They should be abolished. All you have to do is think of ways to cook them afterwards. I like to give people substantial food, particularly when they're drinking—a ham or roast beef, great cheeses and homemade breads, a gutsy pâté (page 176). The most popular hors d'oeuvre I've ever served is kielbasa, a Polish sausage, poached in red wine and shallots and sliced on the bias." An ideal cocktail party menu would include all of these plus the trimmings for roast beef sandwiches.

Occasionally, for drinks at summer parties he may prepare a "Governor of Tahiti's Punch"—by inserting a bruised vanilla bean in a bottle of medium rum (Bacardi or Mount Gay) twenty-four hours in advance of the party. When guests arrive, the mysteriously flavored rum is poured over crushed ice in champagne glasses and garnished with a slice of lime. In winter he likes hot grog. Too often, he finds, are non-drinkers neglected by hosts. In summer he provides them with iced tea or lemonade with a blush of cassis, in winter, spiced tomato juice.

An inveterate traveler and partygoer, Mr. Beard observes that the standard cocktail party hours are six-thirty to nine in New York, whereas five to seven-thirty or eight is more usual elsewhere. He claims that the most successful New Year's Eve party he ever gave took off at the unlikely hour of five in the afternoon. Guests, who were invited to come straight from work, were served Scotch, champagne and nutmeg-dusted milk punch (which he prefers to eggnog) served in old-fashioned glasses. Everyone was out by eight, Jim recalls with satisfaction. On the delicate matter of drawing a party to a merry end, Mr. Beard concludes on a helpful note—serving coffee, he advises, possibly with a little box of imported biscuits, is the most genial way to hint to guests that the moment to leave is at hand. "As any showman will tell you," he once wrote, "there is no greater reward than pleasing your audience."

priscilla morgan

Priscilla Morgan is a *salonière* in the great European tradition. Her good friends are both legion and legend—Isamu Noguchi, Samuel Barber, Buckminster Fuller, Willem de Kooning, Arthur Penn, Gian Carlo Menotti, Richard Lindner, Sir Roland and Lady Penrose, to mention but a few: "Mixing people from different worlds and age groups gives nonstop energy to a party." But Priscilla's continued success as a hostess is a matter of more than guest list mechanics: she has the gift of gathering the creative and the serious without sacrificing gaiety. Above all, she likes to introduce people whom she feels might one day influence, or in some way help, each other: "I'm for parties which end with guests feeling that they've gained something, discovered something, *learned* something!"

Has she any magic formulae for successfully mixing people? "Yes. If you give in to Can I bring so and so?' it can cast a terrible pall at a party. Even at a cocktail party I discourage it. And I always make sure to invite a few beautiful women," she adds with a wicked glint. "Jealous wives add a certain dramatic energy to any party."

A tireless director of the Spoleto Festival for many years, Priscilla not only managed to bring fresh creative talent to a discerning audience but helped secure regular funding for that annual cultural event and fearlessly shouldered the responsibilities of hostess to visiting sponsors and stars: "At one point or other, I have had to do everything—make the beds, sleep in the fields." Priscilla's approach to entertaining either at home or abroad is that of the aesthetic purist; unfailingly, her surroundings and parties bear eloquent testimony to Mies van der Rohe's dictum that "less is more."

atmosphere

Priscilla's apartment is decorated with sparse elegance: white walls and high ceilings, a Ficus tree pruned into a giant umbrella, a huge Victorian table, ringed by carved Belter chairs—all a perfect background to set off Noguchi sculpture and Lindner paintings. At dinner, the living-dining room is bathed in the soft glow of Noguchi's akari light sculptures. The great Japanese-American artist has convinced Priscilla that candlelight is not a twentieth-century form of illumination ("therefore false"); in any case, "I prefer to see my guests." On the table, napkins of various contrasting solid colors echo a large bouquet of mixed blossoms, rarely two alike. Priscilla, who selects them herself at a friendly florist's according to the season, tries always to include daisies, "which are the center of my life," and powerfully perfumed tuberoses "because they remind me of Rome."

food and drink

"Simple dishes such as plain boiled beef or chicken come as a great surprise to people who are used to going out to a lot of dinner parties," says Priscilla. "Everyone seems to enjoy them whether they're dieting or not. With limited time and space I'm not tempted to experiment all over the place. The kitchen is an extension of my office, so I like it to be visually perfect. This means a drastically pared down *batterie de cuisine*. But with simple food you don't need a lot of complicated equipment. I find a blender's the only gadget that's indispensable. And Teflon pots and pans, which help keep the extra pounds away. Then you need only a spin-dryer for salad—the secret of good salad is getting each leaf bone-dry—a spatula, a garlic press, a few good sharp knives, a big stockpot, a fish poacher, and a decent oven and broiler. A few herbs, garlic, kosher salt, black pepper mill and plenty of lemons, and I'm all set for simple fresh food, simply seasoned, simply cooked. And let us not forget some lovely Italian wines and really good bread."

Here is a typical Priscilla Morgan dinner menu:

> Boiled brisket of beef with carrots, leeks, pars-
> nips, celery and turnips
> Warm horseradish sauce
> Green salad with garlic dressing
> Cheese platter (Port Salut, Chèvre and bleu or
> Roquefort) with French bread and Carr's water
> biscuits or Bremers crackers
> Berries in season
> Wine: Valpolicella or Bardolino
> Espresso and Liqueurs: Cognac and Cointreau

Priscilla explains that "being brought up on the banks of the Hudson has made me a fanatic about fresh seasonal food. In springtime, I could eat asparagus and shad roe every other night. Or poached salmon or soft-shell crabs. You just can't go wrong with simple dishes. With some highly sophisticated friends, if I don't have boiled chicken with cups of broth every time they come, I can see their faces fall—no, *plummet*." She is also justly famous for her salads; once again, the trick is simplicity: "The very best Italian olive oil, a little kosher salt, a few grinds of black pepper, a half squeeze of the garlic press and, most important, no more than a *hair* of Spice Island tarragon or wine vinegar beaten up in the bottom of the salad bowl. For greens I like a combination of Boston lettuce, endive, watercress, and the crisp inner leaves of romaine. Sometimes in the dead of winter I buy a dessert, maybe an excellent apple pie to reheat before serving. Otherwise I stick to simple fruit—oranges in Cointreau, strawberries in zabaglione sauce, which is simply egg yolks, sugar and marsala beaten together over heat."

peter and cathy morrell

Peter Morrell is one of New York's most enthusiastic and knowledgeable young wine merchants. He and his wife, Cathy, whose professional interest lies in the theater, entertain in a manner which reflects their common passion for fine food and wines. "We're a do-it-yourself couple," says Cathy. "It runs in the family. If you're clever and prepare in advance, it's easy."

preferences

Small dinners focused upon what the great nineteenth-century gastronome Brillat-Savarin defined as "the pleasures of the table," which, he explained, differ from the elementary pleasures of eating in that they "are known only to the human race; they depend on careful preparations for the serving of the meal, on the choice of place, and on the thoughtful assembling of the guests . . ."

The Morrells also like to give an occasional wine-tasting. "We've never given a cocktail party. Not that we haven't tried—we wrote ten guest lists, but somehow never had it."

atmosphere

Stepping through the doorway of the Morrell's airy white penthouse one recognizes immediately that this is the domain of dedicated wine lovers. Racks, shelves and tables positively glitter with bottles, decanters, crystal and glassware. The wall between the dining room and high ceilinged kitchen has been reduced to a broad archway spanning low built-in cupboards, the tops of which can serve as auxiliary service areas. This arrangement allows the host and hostess, who frequently "take turns with courses," to go about their business without conversational interruption. In fair weather, champagne is served as an apéritif on a rose-entwined, canopied terrace high above the East River and United Nations complex. The host, who invariably wears a sommelier's chain and silver tasting cup around his neck, pours the champagne with infectious gusto rather than solemn professional reverence.

food and drink

"Wine," Peter candidly points out, "is like any other hobby. First you run around getting all the equipment. Then, after a while, you can finally settle down and start to enjoy yourself." His advice to untutored hosts is refreshingly straightforward and simple. For inexpensive entertaining he claims that California jug wines are constantly improving. Pressed to choose a favorite, he singles out Sebastian Cabernet Sauvignon or Pinot Chardonnay. He also considers the Zinfandel "a great entertaining grape" and prefers the Inglenook label.

For those who want to become involved with wine on a grander scale, Peter suggests investing in "an ideal wine cellar," a self-instructive sampling of forty-eight bottles housed in a rack, the design of which is unimportant.

The forty-eight-bottle wine rack can be found on page 56. The initial cost, Peter assures us, is well worth it. "I'd certainly make the investment once. This way you have forty-eight bottles of good wine at your disposal. You can keep the rack or racks in a closet or on display. I ordinarily tap my rack for the two of us or when friends drop by and then fill in the holes as soon as I get around to it. It's a good way to familiarize yourself with a wide range of wine. It's also a good idea to keep a scrapbook of labels with comments—you get a visual picture of what you want in the future."

For dinner parties Peter recommends buying for the particular evening. Magnums, in that they mean half as many corks to pull, are good for parties of all sorts. He likes Macon Blanc, Brouilly, red bordeaux and burgundies. Larger than magnum-sized champagne bottles, he warns, can create problems, as they are difficult to handle and chill. Two half-sized bottles of champagne are always kept at the ready in his refrigerator for spontaneous celebrations—"These stories about having to chill champagne just before serving it are nonsense—it will be damaged only if frozen. But forget those small splits—they're *terrible*."

Peter advises that wine-tasting parties make sense only for a relatively large number of people. "You get ten good tastes to the bottle, so obviously if you want to present a wide and interesting variety either you have to invite a lot of tasters or waste a good deal of wine." A wine-tasting is an unusual way to entertain, both easy and inexpensive compared, for example, to giving a big cocktail-buffet party. Count noses and choose roughly half as many bottles as you have guests. While you can try the hit-or-miss technique, a leisurely conference with your dealer will help you select a more interestingly balanced range. The bottles of wine, possibly accompanied by tent cards giving the vital statistics of each, are left open on a table along with plenty of wine glasses—Peter prefers lightweight to heavy crystal. He suggests two basic shapes to see you through all occasions—a classic stemmed wine glass with fairly straight sides for reds and a fluted or tulip-shaped stemmed glass for whites and champagnes.

As far as food is concerned, the tasters' hands must not be encumbered with plates; it's

best simply to set out little cubes of cheese on toothpicks—muenster, Gruyère, cheddar. Strong or crumbly cheeses, like Rocquefort, are either difficult to handle or overpower the lighter wines. Thin slices of French bread or a mild flavored cracker help clear the palate between tastings.

At dinner, Peter's general rule of thumb is one bottle of wine for every two people. When four sat down to table, it was traditional to serve one bottle of white wine with the first course, and one bottle of red with the main course, particularly if it was red meat. These distinctions are not always observed now, even in France, where it is not uncommon to drink the same white or red throughout the meal. Certainly the more common practice in America is to serve one wine with the meal. The weather should be taken into consideration; a chilled white is lighter and more refreshing in summer; a full-bodied red, more soul-satisfying in winter. In the final analysis, you can always bow to personal taste.

If it is to be decanted, red wine should be poured out slowly one to two hours before dinner, taking care that no sediment escapes from the bottom of the bottle. If it is to be served in its bottle, uncork the same length of time in advance and rest the cork on its side over the opening—this will permit sufficient air to enter for the wine to "breathe" properly.

When there are six diners, a third bottle may be introduced in the form of a dessert wine, such as a good sauterne. Dessert wines make a delightful conclusion to a meal and should be more widely enjoyed than they are at present. The Morrells' guests are always treated to the very best wines (which are not necessarily the most expensive) whether they are connoisseurs or not—"The highest compliment we can pay our friends is to assume that they will enjoy a fine wine."

Here is a typical dinner served by the Morrells:

Asparagus vinaigrette
Onion soup   Montrachet 1969
Scallops of veal in caper sauce
Green salad   Ridge Zinfandel, Lytton Springs, 1972
Roquefort and French bread
Crème Caramel   Sylvaner Beerenauslese
Coffee and liqueurs

In this instance, Cathy will have prepared everything but the meat course ahead of time. The veal itself will be cooked and served by Peter, once the soup dishes are cleared away. Cheerily unflappable, he manages to deftly sauté, season and stir while carrying on nonstop dialogues with the guests.

Cathy holds down a full-time job, and so she has become expert at devising menus that can be prepared entirely in advance. One favorite is:

Cold carrot vichysoisse
Coq au vin on crouton triangles
Endive and watercress salad with mustard vinaigrette
Homemade cheesecake with strawberries

With eight guests waiting for this meal, she need merely to pop the coq au vin and croutons in the oven to reheat and to dress the salad with a premixed vinaigrette sauce.

As enthusiastic as he is about wine, Peter also is fond of fine liquors and liqueurs. His basic bar is stocked with premium Scotches, Beefeater or Tanqueray gin, Jack Daniels sour mash, Mount Gay rum, Spanish sherries and Bossière vermouth, which he thinks makes the best martinis. Stolichnaya vodka is kept in the freezer. An extra tip: uncorked vermouth, sherry and other fortified wines and commercial apéritifs such as Dubonnet tend to eventually "go off"—ninety days is about their maximum life expectancy once they've been opened. After that they may become cloudy, musty and sour.

For after-dinner liqueurs the Morrells like Cognac, Armagnac, the newly popular almond-based Italian Amaretto, Galliano, and the clear, dry fruit brandies of France and Switzerland such as Poire (pear), Framboise (raspberry) and Mirabelle (of the plum family). Peter pleads that port be included in the after-dinner drink category; sometimes he serves it as liqueur-cum-dessert by poaching sweetened apricots and peaches in port and flaming them with brandy, a dramatic finale that takes only five minutes from start to finish: "If you really want to go wild with calories, you can top the whole thing off with ice cream." Such temptations, at the Morrells', seem a permanent condition.

lee traub

Throughout the week, both Lee and Marvin Traub lead bracingly busy lives in Manhattan, he as president of Bloomingdale's, she as president of the New York Dance Alliance, an agency offering technical and organizational assistance to professional dance companies. The parents of two sons and a daughter, all of them about college age, the Traubs cherish the relative quiet of life in Westchester, where they spend most of their nights and weekends in a serenely welcoming house splendidly suited to relaxed entertaining.

preferences

Easy Sunday lunches for family and friends in the sunny, glassed-in conservatory room overlooking the garden. Garden picnics seated on the grass for six to eight. For the evening, Lee prefers "to think in terms of 'having friends over' rather than 'dinner parties.' I love company, but I don't like big, impersonal, pay-back evenings. I far prefer informal, seemingly casual entertaining, unless I can find some handle which will pick a party up and make it something out of the ordinary. This might be music or decorations—sometimes the food alone can do it. To me, 'small' for lunch means something different from 'small' for dinner. Whereas lunch might be for just six or eight, dinner will usually be for at least twelve or fourteen. And if I'm going to the effort to prepare an elaborate buffet, then we'll invite at least twenty-four."

food and drink

Lee has approached entertaining with the same professional wisdom that would guide any capable dance-company director—she has systematically built up a sound basic repertoire. Like many other hostesses she keeps a detailed record of guest lists, menus, decorations, etc.; however, she makes additional observations where others leave off, specifically, how much of what was eaten and how much was not: "By recording your culinary success and failures, you start to build your own foolproof repertory."

Sunday lunches, for example: "I honestly enjoy the preparation of lunch. I generally gravitate toward chicken, because everybody always likes it. I've worked out about five or six basic menus with variations—depending on what I find in the garden or the refrigerator. All are served with extraordinary amounts of wine and end with fresh espresso."

Lunch I: Poached, boned chicken breasts served at room temperature with a pesto or "green" sauce of blended fresh (and possibly dried) herbs, oil, a spark of fresh lemon juice, a mite of Dijon mustard, salt and freshly ground pepper. With this would be served crisp French bread ("or any other interesting bread from Bloomie's Bread Basket"), a little green salad, and, for dessert, pound cake (see page 202).

Lunch II: Madhur Jaffrey's marinated broiled chicken (page 192), a salad of mozzarella, fresh tomatoes, coarsely chopped basil and oil, crisp bread.

Lunch III: Salad of cubed poached chicken, green seedless grapes and sliced water chestnuts in curried mayonnaise sharpened with lemon juice ("You can do the same with tuna and canned unsweetened green grapes for a real hurry-up lunch made exclusively from things which can be kept on hand in the larder.") With this Lee likes sliced tomatoes with basil and heated bread.

Lunch IV: "I guess you could call this one 'Lee Traub's Ostentatious Chef's Salad.' We eat it in one variation or another by the carload. I start putting things in, and before I know it I've enough to feed the whole neighborhood." A typical chef's salad fantasy à la Lee might include bite-sized greens of as many varieties she can lay hands on, diced or julienne chicken, ham, thinly sliced leftover steak or London broil, cherry tomatoes, "sun-chokes," steamed broccoli flowerets, artichoke hearts, wild rice, Gruyère, mozzarella (or Caerfilly), sliced raw mushrooms and shavings of carrot doused with a vinaigrette and tossed only at the last moment. The various ingredients nestling in separate clumps on a cushion of broken greens gives the effect of a sumptuous mosaic. Hot Southern-style drop biscuits are recommended as an accompaniment. A plain cake is all that need follow.

Lunch V: "The children used to call this kind of lunch an orgy—what could be more soul-satisfying than several kinds of the best cheese, with a lot of fresh bread, wine and fruit? Eaten on the grass, it's an unbeatable menu."

More elaborate picnics *chez Traub* will include "a good pâté or terrine, some kind of cold meat—roast chicken, a smoky ham or wurst, a cold curried rice salad with pignoli and currants, and cold, lightly cooked and marinated vegetables. Watermelon slices and homemade brownies make a perfect dessert."

And what about those special parties where food is "the handle"? "I adore Indian cuisine and Danish 'cold tables.' Each is marvelous for big parties because it provides a dramatic change of pace and, better still, almost everything can be prepared in advance. I swear by Madhur Jaffrey's book (see page 95). Although Indian food is an awful lot of work, once you've made it everyone seems to love it. I like a lot of strange things that other people stay away from. And yet I'm always surprised how easily they capitulate, once you've introduced them forcibly. Like the sitar concert we arranged for a late

Sunday afternoon. Three Indian musicians spread carpets as a stage for themselves in front of the fireplace, and thirty guests sat down obediently in chairs we'd set up. I was particularly worried about certain husbands who I was sure would hate the music. I doubt if any of them had been to an authentic Indian buffet, let alone an authentic Indian concert. Well, I can't tell you what a success it was. They kept applauding for more. Nothing could have made us happier than to bring something absolutely new to people's lives. Afterwards, the Indian food kept the mood at the same exciting pitch. The moral is, if you yourself love something unusual, it's worth the risk to try and share it with your friends.

"The same is true of our Danish cold-table parties, which we started to give years before most people knew anything about them. Helping yourself from a great, colorful variety of food is something everyone finds fun. The Danes design superb posters. We hang a few about the dining room walls for atmosphere and guide our friends around the table. You need two glasses with Scandinavian food—one for beer and another tiny, cordial-sized one for chilled akvavit—as well as two plates, the first for the fish course, a second for meats and cheeses. This means sufficient tables must be set up for each guest to have a place to put everything down."

Here is a bountiful Traub Danish cold-table menu:

First course ("gently instruct guests that the fish should be taken first and separately"):

> Salmon mousse
> Herring, beet and apple salad
> Curried herring
> Herring in sour cream with thinly sliced MacIntosh
>   apples and Bermuda onions
> Bloomingdale's smoked eel
> Lobster salad
> Danish baby shrimp (frozen or in jars)

Second Course (on clean plates):

> Sliced Polish ham
> Thin slices of charcoal-broiled London broil (at
>   room temperature)
> Swiss Bundnerfleisch
> Pâté

Saucissons en croûte

Swedish meatballs (the one hot dish; serve in flame-heated casserole or chafing dish)

Dilled cucumber and green bean salad (page 184)

Mushroom salad (page 184)

Hearts of palm (Lee: "Because I love them")

Mixed cooked vegetables in curried mayonnaise

Artichoke salad (with cold rice, capers, pignoli and chopped green pepper)

Two cheeses, such as Danish camembert and bleu

A variety of breads, including pumpernickel and Scandinavian flat bread

Dessert: Almond cookies, espresso.

To serve akvavit as the Danes do, buy a giant-sized can of tomato or other fruit juice. Remove the top and pour the contents into another container. Wash the can well. Place a fifth of imported akvavit into the empty can. Center the bottle carefully. Fill the can with water to the bottom of the bottle neck. Freeze. When ready to serve, remove the bottom of the can with an opener, run the can briefly under hot water and slide out the ice-encased bottle of liquor. Wrap it in a fresh white linen towel and pour off into small cordial glasses. Drink with Danish beer chasers.

When all is said and done, the star performer in Lee's repertoire, however, is her mother's celebrated "Schaum Torte" (page 199), a delicious, chewy, festive-looking meringue cake that one bakes in a spring form pan, slices in half, and fills and decorates as tradition, the season or whim demands. "It is, as all my friends say, 'simply heaven.'"

count and countess guy de brantes

The Count and Countess Guy de Brantes inhabit a comfortable town house just off Fifth Avenue, and they love to fill it with guests. Marina has no servants to assist her, but she is able to entertain up to a hundred people thanks to her own most unusual staff—her children, Emmanuel (eleven), Francois (thirteen) and Pia (fifteen).

preferences

Dinners, brunches, lunches, picnics, birthday parties. Once Marina starts inviting guests, she can't resist including any friend she may run into on the street; in consequence, a small dinner for ten frequently swells to a party for sixty.

atmosphere

Marina (who has recently become one of New York's most sought-after caterers and cooking instructors) explains that she entertains irregularly. When she does, it will always be for a reason, for a special occasion, whether it's a state visit from Guy's sister, Mme. Giscard d'Estaing, or simply to enjoy the full moon in their garden on a balmy summer night. She might give six parties in a row, or none for several months. Although dinners are usually served buffet style on the chopping-block table of her professionally equipped rustic kitchen, guests will find round tables at which to sit comfortably in other rooms of the house. Tables are often covered with brightly patterned sheets—"attractive, fun, easy to clean"—with simple linen napkins of a harmonizing color. Marina prefers glass candelabra and table decorations that are edible, such as mints or glacé fruits.

When the De Brantes entertain, it is always with imagination. Upon entering the drawing room, for example, guests might be handed a slip of paper inscribed with one line of a couplet. Their dinner partner of the evening will be given the second line. Recently, Marina was momentarily alarmed to discover that she had somehow invited no less than a hundred people to an anniversary dinner. Her inspired solution, assisted by her children, was to pack a hundred bags for a mammoth indoor picnic. Included in the assorted delicacies cosseted in individual plastic containers were:

Pâté campagne (page 176)
Slices of roast pork stuffed with prunes
Cold roast beef
Grilled chicken
Hard boiled eggs
Crudités
French bread
Brie

A gala anniversary cake was served separately. As usual, a place had been set for each guest at tables stocked with plenty of wine, salt, pepper and other similar amenities.

Customarily, when guests arrive, the children open the door, greet them and take their coats. They pass hors d'oeuvres and tend bar. This last occupation is a favorite with the boys, who have become expert at mixing generous drinks. Only rarely does an error occur, as when Francois, asked to produce a dry Martini, very logically filled his guest's glass with Martini and Rossi dry vermouth. The children do not set the tables, but they clear them, load and man the dishwasher, and clean up as guests leave the table. For these efforts they are paid a respectable five dollars each. Needless to say, they have earned the boundless admiration of the De Brantes' friends, who now not only invite them to serve at their parties, but send their own children to "apprentice" with Emmanuel, Francois and Pia.

food and drink

Marina's menus are often rather elaborate, as befits a hostess with a trained staff. She feels that Americans and Europeans do not necessarily appreciate the same succession of courses. Americans usually don't wish to be served eggs or soup as a first course because they've often eaten the former at breakfast and the latter at lunch. Europeans, however, and particularly the French, are happy with either; like Guy, most think that dinner isn't really dinner without soup. New Yorkers like their main course followed by salad and cheese served on the same plate. For the French, this is blasphemy. Salad must be served on a side dish, usually with the main course; the cheese, with bread, will be served as a course in itself. The French, "because they are very gourmand," expect a rich and elaborate dessert, such as a mousse with petits fours, a hot dessert soufflé or crêpes. American friends, on the other hand, prefer something fruity and light, such as a tart, a sorbet or an ice cream. A typical meal, tailored to the tastes of European guests;

Watercress soup
Canard à l'orange or aux raisins (page 191)
Wild rice
Salad
Cheese
The Children's Chocolate Mousse (page 200)

Marina will see that the first and last courses are prepared the day before, the main course will be cooked early in the afternoon of the day itself.

The children not only serve at the De Brantes parties, but put a good deal of effort into preparing the food as well. All three are at home in the kitchen. When asked how her children became such prodigies, Marina explains that they are the heirs to a lengthy family tradition. Her own father learned to cook so that he could work on his father's yacht, and has been enthusiastically happy in the kitchen ever since. Marina, whose mother cannot boil proverbial water, learned the secrets of cuisine at her father's knee; today her recipe books are studded with entries such as "Daddy's paella."

For watercress or other soups, the children will peel the vegetables and purée them in the blender, although the actual measuring and seasoning will be handled by Marina. The canard à l'orange or aux raisins (duck with orange or green grapes) which is preferred "crisp, in the American way," is too complicated a dish for the children, but they do cut the oranges into "baskets" and separate the fruit segments. The chocolate mousse they will make unassisted. Marina finds that the children love to make desserts (because they like to lick the bowls), and their repertoire includes cakes, brownies and charlottes, as well as the preparation of the fruit (but not the making of the pastry or pastry cream) for tarts. Above all, credit is always given the children for whatever work they've done. When a buffet dinner is arranged on the kitchen table, little labels inform the guests that, among other things, they are consuming "Francois' Brownies" or "The Children's Chocolate Mousse."

And how do the extraordinary De Brantes children entertain their own friends? There

are several family traditions where birthdays are concerned. It has been silently decreed that Marina must always bake and decorate the cake; not only must it be a surprise, but nevermore repeated: "Pia's Chinese year I tried to construct a pagoda-shaped cake—it was a nightmare." The birthday child has not to be troubled with any of the preparation for his party himself, and each will decide exactly how friends are to be entertained. The formulas they have evolved are fascinating evocations of the bent that each young but firm character has developed. Pia always entertains at home. There will be boys and girls and music for dancing. Each year the food will be chosen from a different national source: a seven-foot-long Italian hero, a Chinese feast, sent from a restaurant, or Grandfather's paella. Francois, on the other hand, entertains only boys and likes to go out. A day at the movies with buddies is considered ideal, and if dinner is served at home, lasagna will be perfect. But whatever they do, says Marina, they have to come home and eat *that cake*.

bruce sinclair

Bruce Sinclair, bachelor food critic and cassette producer, has devised a shrewdly organized yet seemingly casual way in which to entertain guests at a beach house too small for overnight weekend guests.

preferences

Six to eight guests for a full day and evening by the ocean. Bruce has worked out a schedule whereby he greets friends at the morning ferry with a pitcher of Bloody Marys. The same night he shepherds them safely back onto the last boat for the mainland, groggily content from a day in the sun and fresh air, punctuated with rounds of excellent food and drink.

atmosphere

To give his house a clean, uncluttered look, Bruce sticks to a strict color scheme of yellows, oranges, hot pink and terra cotta, set off against a background of stark white. Everything immediately harmonizes, from the paper napkins, linens, candles, and dishes to the decorative hanging banners, towels, cushions, captain's chairs and luxuriant marigolds in clay pots set out on tables and sun decks.

Bruce says that at the beach a house must be guest-proofed for the sake of maintenance as well as unscathed bare feet—a deckpainted floor, washable Spanish bedspreads as carpets from which tar stains can be removed, indestructible enameled tinware bowls and plates, stemless wine glasses, which will not tip over and break (for all drinks, Bruce stocks only highball and old-fashioned sizes), stainless flatware, stacks of paper napkins, and because glasses sweat profusely by the sea, coasters scattered everywhere.

Bruce is well equipped to answer his guests' needs. In the bathroom he keeps an abundance of huge beach towels, as well as Band-Aids, sun lotions and mosquito repellent. By the front door an amusing collection of sun hats is displayed along with slickers for guests to wear for rainy-day walks on the beach. Their host assures us that they will inevitably return with pockets bulging full of stones, shells and starfish, all of which will be abandoned on his premises when the day is done.

As rainy days at the beach call for intensive consolation, an emergency reserve of games and other divertissements is essential. Backgammon and cards head the preferred list; Bruce leans to bouts of "Spite and Malice," a sort of cutthroat card version of backgammon. Whatever is played, a basic rule book of common games is good to have on hand to settle unseemly arguments. Bruce suggests jigsaw puzzles for those *in extremis*, but charades only if there are eight people who honestly like charades. If the weather permits, the all-time favorite amusement is clamming. When everyone returns to the house, Bruce sits guests down on a deck (there are two, designed so that on a clear day one will always be able to choose between sun and shade), hands them scrub brushes and openers and lets them go to work.

Taped background music, running to Handel and Vivaldi, plays almost without inter-

91

ruption, covering abrupt lulls in the conversation and enabling the host to retreat to his kitchen alone, secure in the knowledge that the guests have something to occupy their attention. "When you're playing master of ceremonies literally from morning to night, you have to feel that occasionally you can—and *must*—divorce yourself from the guests and take a breather. Otherwise it begins to seem like too much work, which makes you resentful and spells death for the party.

food and drink

"People arrive hungry after the trip and in need of something solid, so I have hot sandwiches—*Croque Monsieurs* (page 177—waiting for them in an electric frying pan—I haul out the ice bucket, refill the trays, and tell everybody to help themselves. That electric frying pan has to be one of the greatest inventions in the world. Unlike the stove, it keeps things warm without heating up the place. Also, a blender and a charcoal grill are the salvation for a summer house. Cold soups can be made in a minute and grilling out on the deck keeps you away from a sweltering kitchen."

To be able to enjoy the day along with the guests, he prepares most of the meals before they arrive. Note the plural—meals. The Bloody Mary and *Croque Monsieur* breakfast is followed by a relaxed period of sunning, swimming, sipping drinks and nibbling chilled raw vegetables. Lunch itself will not be served until about three P.M., giving everyone enough time on the beach without being themselves fried to a crisp. If they must leave early, it will be a hearty lunch; a lighter menu will be served if they are staying for dinner and the late ferry.

In the latter case, a favorite light lunch menu might include:

> Cold meat salad, either with vinaigrette sauce or
>   mayonnaise
> Marinated string beans
> French bread
> Wild blueberries (picked by the guests from
>   bushes behind the house) with homemade
>   *crème fraiche*.

Drinks may be served later in the afternoon with a hard cheese (New York State Cheddar seems to keep well at the beach) and more crudités. Late dinner served an hour before departure must be "simple, delicious and filling" for those by now drunk with sun and good cheer.

Pasta with fresh pesto
Charcoal-grilled shish kebabs
Green salad

Bruce finds a meat salad "an ideal cook-ahead dish." He marinates a London broil in oil, vinegar and Worcestershire sauce overnight and broils it the day before guests arrive. The next day it is carved into thin 1" to 2" pieces and combined with salad greens, tomatoes and hard boiled eggs sauced with a tangy vinaigrette or fresh herbed mayonnaise whipped up in the blender, usually with basil from the herb garden. To vary the mayonnaise, he might add a little hot pepper, mustard, capers or green peppercorns.

Potted shrimp is another quick and easy specialty—coarsely chopped, freshly boiled shrimp are stuffed into little pots, *completely* covered (this is important) with clarified butter and stored in the refrigerator; this is excellent spread on toast as an hors d'oeuvre or first course. On the long, squat, heavy grill, Bruce cooks chicken with fresh tarragon from the garden and whole sea bass rubbed with olive oil and clamped in a long-handled turner, its cavity seasoned with salt, pepper and a generous bath of lemon juice. Bruce keeps frozen chicken stock on hand to blend with vegetable purées for easy summer soups. A favorite mingles puréed carrot, heavy cream, chicken stock, nutmeg and a sprinkling of parsley. Basil from the garden is converted into pungent *pesto alla Genovese* (page 187) and stored in the refrigerator as an instant pasta sauce. When other perishable or home-frozen foods have been prepared in the city, he brings them to the beach packed in insulated bags, swathed heavily in newspaper.

Bruce stocks his self-service bar with house brand gin and vodka (he also keeps "the good stuff for martinis"), Campari, sweet and dry vermouths, and summer mixers—soda, tonic, bitter lemon. Spritzers are always popular thirst-quenchers; for these he decants Almadén Chablis into handsome crystal flasks. Red wine is transported weekly, as it cannot withstand the heat of the house when it is closed up (neither can candles—they are stashed in the refrigerator during the week).

He objects to only three kinds of guests: those who persist in trying to help ("No one can do my dishes as well as I can"), guests who tarry on the beach when lunch is ready, and those too inebriated to leave. On the secret of good entertaining, he has this to say: "Never over or underdo—drinks too weak or too strong, menus too short or too long, helpings too gross or too meager, tables bare of essential plates and ash trays, or so cluttered the guest is unable to maneuver. Perfection comes with common sense and balance."

94

madhur jaffrey

Madhur Jaffrey, born in New Delhi, makes her home in New York with her husband, Sanford Allen, a violinist with the New York Philharmonic, and her three teen-aged daughters. She has enjoyed a career as an actress of major importance in India, and she now instructs Americans in the delicious mysteries of her native cuisine. She is the author of *An Invitation to Indian Cooking* and an invitation to Madhur's table is the envy of those New Yorkers who have learned to appreciate the nuances of authentic Indian food.

preferences

Seated dinners for six, or for ten or twelve guests at the most, and buffet-style suppers. She mixes ages from ten to ninety, and is unconcerned about even numbers. The emphasis at her parties is "always on food."

atmosphere

Madhur Jaffrey sinks gently into the cushions of her Greenwich Village apartment. An Indian mattress covered in indigos, corals, pinks and golds, and piled with

95

spangled pillows stretches invitingly along the floor. A second one cushions the wall behind. Or if you'd rather, you may settle back into the recesses of a large carved Victorian sofa. This and similarly massive pieces of Victoriana impose themselves like giant English visitors among their sari-swathed owner's Oriental brassbound chests, sculpture, wall hangings, metal boxes and exquisite coral lacquer work.

Madhur describes a wedding feast for a thousand in her native northern India. Colorful cotton rugs are spread on the floor, over which long runner sheets are unwound as tablecloths for the squatting guests, who dine off disposable plates made of leaves pinned together with twigs. Food is offered by servants bearing three dishes at a time. The guests are obliged by etiquette to refuse, not once but twice, secure in the knowledge that they will be served anyway despite their polite and hollow protestations.

How does Madhur adapt her native customs to the dictates of Western entertaining? If there are only six guests, they will be served at the table, and service will be in the traditional Indian style. Each guest is seated before a large platterlike round plate, approximately eighteen inches in diameter. Madhur's are of stainless steel, but silver or brass would be customary in India. Around the rim of this plate are clustered small, round bowls filled with various vegetables and meat dishes. A banana leaf or small plate brightened by various chutneys and condiments will also be placed at the rim. If a plate is used it will be of glass, as "nothing sour is ever placed on metal." At the center of the large plate, breads, rice, dumplings or fritters are arranged.

If more than six guests have been invited Madhur will serve them in the manner of a Western buffet supper. Glass bowls and plates permit the lovely glowing colors of the food to be admired, but she also has an irrepressible urge to buy ceramics whenever they appeal to her. Accordingly, beans are cooked and served in a handsome terracotta pot, and a collection of small serving bowls and miniature vases sprout single flowers beside each plate at seated dinners.

Madhur's Victorian table, dressed with a cloth and napkins printed in India, is always radiant with flowers—anemones, peonies, lilacs, iris. Indeed, they are an indispensible aspect of life—"I was brought up in a home with fourteen gardens, and didn't realize that vegetables or flowers could be bought until I was thirteen."

She enthusiastically embraces many Western notions, including such time-saving electrical appliances as a blender, mixer, processor, broiler, rotisserie, hot cart, one coffee grinder for crushing spices and another to fulfill its original purpose. An Eastern custom which has been gratefully discarded is the murderously elaborate menu: "I used to cook seven or eight vegetables plus chicken, meat and a fish. I thought that was the way you had to do it. I'd been brought up to feel that *that* was a party. But no longer."

Above all, Madhur feels, the atmosphere at her dinners must be relaxed. Dinner hour is late; guests are invited for eight o'clock, but the meal itself is not served until between nine and nine-thirty. Guests are encouraged to wear "comfortable clothes." It does not disturb her if a person sits quietly, without speaking—in fact, "sometimes a very quiet evening is nice when friends have been nervous or exhausted." Conversation must come naturally. She is not adamant about a guest's ability to entertain others, although she admits wistfully that "there are some people who bore everybody."

food and drink

Madhur, whose kitchen space is limited, plans her meals two days in advance so that marinating and pre-cooking can be done at leisure. She finds shopping daily both "comforting and relaxing" and hates to order by phone: "I see these orders go out and marvel at people's trusting natures." At present she is compiling a vegetarian cookbook, which accounts for the somewhat botanical nature of the buffet menu she was contemplating when last we spoke:

First course (served as hors d'oeuvres with drinks):

Chick peas and green beans
(with garlic and spices, served cold)
Tomatoes stuffed with kheema
(spiced and gingery chopped lamb)

Main course:
Stuffed eggplant
Cauliflower and potatoes cooked with fennel,
    cumin and black onion seed
Yogurt flavored with chopped mint
Bhatura (fried bread)

Dessert: Kulfi (an ice cream made of reduced milk
    flavored with pistachio and cardamom)

This particular meal probably will be served with beer. Rare wines are Sanford's special interest, but both agree that the subtleties of a French vintage would be lost when confronted with an array of vibrantly spiced Indian dishes.

Madhur and Sanford, both night people, normally stay up until two or three in the morning. Nothing pleases them more than the company of a few friends who remain to chat after others leave. As a final Indian touch, departing guests are offered, as a *digestif,* fennel seeds, cardamom, betel nuts and whole cloves kept in the tiny compartments of an antique Paan box. When the last visitor has left, all the dishes are packed in the washing machine—a final Western touch.

Two of Madhur's delicious, easy-to-follow recipes appear on pages 184 and 192. The first she describes as a "fresh relish," the second is for broiled marinated chicken. The two combine marvelously well, and as they can be prepared in advance, they are a boon to relaxed entertaining. They are reprinted from Madhur's fascinating and instructive book, *An Invitation to Indian Cooking,* and most of the other recipes mentioned in her menus can also be found there.

alexis gregory

Alexis Gregory—peripatetic international publisher, linguist, impassioned traveler, art collector, gifted cook and tireless host—entertains with staggering frequency at both his New York apartment and guest-filled house in the Hamptons. A debonair bachelor, he is able to manage equally well single-handedly, with the aid of an old family cook, or with a full complement of hired staff, depending on numbers and the relative formality of the occasion.

preferences

Buffet dinners for as many as sixty guests, seated dinners for eight to twenty-four, large cocktail parties, weekend house parties—"I love to cook in the country, but hate it in the city."

atmosphere

Alex believes strongly in the European custom of mixing family with friends, which creates an immediate air of Russian and Continental charm at his parties. Home in New York is a Fifth Avenue duplex of compact proportions—a large living room, small kitchen and guest lavatory on the first floor, a bed-sitting room and bath on the second. Alex's masterful sense of organization can be seen in his party traffic plans, his various tabletops, each displaying a contrasting period of sculptural art, or for that matter, in the systematic manner with which he approaches even the most trifling of undertakings. He has established rules for himself on all aspects of hospitality. When entertaining weekend guests, Alex is reknowned for his ability to judge to a berry how much food will be consumed. His secret? "What you have, they eat."

On the subject of entertaining in general he is an inexhaustible compendium of succinct theories and tips which are best passed on in his own brisk delivery: 1) "A party is a battle. Lay your strategy in advance and be prepared for the best and worst." 2)

"Enjoy yourself at other people's houses; work at your own." 3) "No matter how occupied you are, always look relaxed."

On *assembling a guest list*: "People are like flowers. You have to arrange a bouquet that fits together. At a dinner, when I mix groups, which I usually do, I'll always invite several members from each so that no one's completely alone. I also try to seat each guest next to one familiar face. If there are two tables or more, I split up all couples. Couples generally tend to be too self-contented—that's why I invite as many singles as possible. However, you should also try to foresee any personality clashes that might flare up, and seat excitable people at separate tables. With small groups it's a bad idea to invite a dominating personality unless whoever it is is unfailingly brilliant and entertaining. As far as collecting even numbers is concerned, I refuse to worry about it. When a man cancels, it's useless to scrounge for a last-minute replacement, because the minute you do the phone will ring and . . . ? It will be a woman saying *she* can't make it."

On *the subject of drinks*: "At a dinner I don't like it when drinks go on too long. Make the drinks strong, unless the wine is going to be very good. If the dinner's going to be excellent, keep junk to the minimum—if it's not so hot, make lots of hors d'oeuvres."

On *dinner and buffets*: "Decide on the degree of formality, but don't go beyond your menus in style by getting overly complicated. If the dinner's going to be served seated, plan on at least three courses. Sometimes it's not a bad idea to serve the first course before going in to dinner. For ten or less, eat at a round table for the sake of conversation. Also, having a guest of honor gets things going. Keep decorations low so everybody can see one another.

"When you place people at a large party, you have to be like a headwaiter and seat the older or more distinguished guests most comfortably. At a buffet I steer the older ones up to the bedroom, where proper tables and chairs are set up. I also stick lost souls into compatible circles—all this needs quick thinking."

On *after-dinner coffee and drinks*: "You can have coffee at or away from the table. Don't make any rules—just decide fast! If conversation's going strong and no guests are arriving later, stay put. But if everybody's either silent or fighting, break it up and hope they all leave the room. A very good French custom is to pass fresh fruit juice and ice water after dinner. Also offer drinks such as champagne or brandy, but not too many liqueurs—one or two choice ones is quite enough. If you're planning some kind of entertainment for after dinner—music, cards, charades or whatever—have a plate of small sandwiches ready to bring out later. It costs little, it seems highly luxurious, and it's also nice for guests who are coming in afterwards."

On *large cocktail parties*: "You can mix guests as freely as you want. You have to try to

fill the room nicely—not too much, not too little—you have to practice to get it straight. I make as many introductions as possible without irritating people, and I keep circling like the shark, who sinks unless he swims. I keep an eye out for lost or unhappy guests and take special care of them, but otherwise talk a bit to everyone. Drinks are long, strong and heavy, hors d'oeuvres are mixed, pretty and lots. A table of hors d'oeuvres is nice because it eliminates forcing a way through people just to pass a plate. If the season's good, an outdoor cocktail party's much better than one indoors. You can put torches in the garden—they're cheap, but very dramatic and give a flattering light."

On the unexpected: "If possible, I try to plot an evening so that something new's happening all the time. Guests coming in after dinner make a kind of second party. Games, like music, are O.K. if the mood's right. Try to prepare a surprise. It can be the food, a little present in each napkin, a musician in the middle of dinner—never at the start; it wastes the impact—a poem read by a guest, an amusing table decoration—you know, something like a girl in a pie."

And finally, there is his ultimate Cardinal Rule: "If everything is clicking, forget the rules and enjoy yourself. You know you are having a success."

carol inouye

Carol Inouye, a young Japanese-American designer and illustrator, introduces what might be called "Japanese home cooking" to an assortment of guests in her small studio apartment.

preferences

Small dinners—seated for four or six; buffets of "finger food" for eight or ten.

Carol tells us that the concept of entertaining at home is totally foreign to the Japanese idea of appropriate hospitality: "The Japanese are so concerned about form. In a way I guess it's good, at least for them." According to ancient tradition, only members of the family are invited to dine in the Japanese home. Nonrelatives are taken to restaurants, tea houses or Geisha establishments. If, on an extremely rare occasion, someone were actually invited into a private house, refreshments would be limited to green tea ("without the ceremony") and a slice of yokan, a solid sweet bean paste. Among exclusively male company, sake might be served, but little else.

atmosphere

Happily for her friends in California and New York, Carol has managed to fuse the traditional East with the contemporary West when she entertains. "Most of the time I give dinners on Friday nights. After all, people do have to go to work—this way they can stay until one or two A.M. without feeling guilty." If no more than four to six are to be fed, a seated dinner will be eaten at table. If a slightly larger number have been invited, Carol will set out a buffet supper on a white Parsons table. Having collected their plates, guests will arrange themselves on tatami mats and huge cushions around "low makeshift coffee tables," a system Carol recommends "for somebody who doesn't have furniture—it's casual, unusual and fun." To heighten the atmosphere, soft Japanese music will be played on the phonograph throughout the evening.

103

The apartment is never illuminated by candles, as "the Japanese have these phobias about fires"—with good reason, as most Japanese houses are still built of wood and furnished with paper screens and straw mats. Furthermore, when the Japanese decorate for a dinner, they decorate the food rather than the table. Visitors to Japan return agog with tales of exorbitant fugu fish presentations in specially licensed restaurants where tissue-paper-thin slices of the fish's flesh are transformed upon each plate into a fantastic bas-relief of a feathered crane in flight. Carol is less ambitious in her endeavors, but always decorates her food with "trees" of fern and sprigs of pine, or with bamboo, parsley and watercress, radishes, carrot curls and cauliflowerets.

food and drink

"Japanese food is very simple," Carol explains, "not oily or greasy, quite bland and probably very healthy. Colors and textures are very important—ideally you should have something soft, something meaty, something crunchy." That the Japanese cuisine runs heavily to seafood is not so surprising when one learns that until a century ago, meat, chicken and eggs were unknown.

When planning a buffet, Carol includes only dishes that can be eaten with the fingers. "It's awkward to eat with chopsticks, sitting on the floor, and with Western friends it's just too painful for me to watch." The menus, despite this limitation, are as delightfully varied as this one:

Japanese Buffet

Sushi rice balls (balls of Japanese rice with raw
    marinated salt-water fish)
Yakitori (boned marinated chicken cubes grilled
    on skewers along with mushrooms, scallions
    and cherry tomatoes; for marinade, see
    page 196)
Seafood and vegetable tempura (page 196)
Tangerines

At smaller seated dinners, Carol will be able to serve: teriyaki, which is sliced chicken or beef steeped in the same marinade as yakitori is, then repeatedly basted as it bakes in a 350° oven until inner pinkness just disappears. The teriyaki is served with plain boiled rice, which, if cooked ahead, can be wrapped in a clean towel and suspended in a sieve over boiling water to reheat. This, Carol would probably team with her favorite salad or cucumber and crabmeat lightly dressed with soy sauce, rice wine vinegar and toasted sesame seeds, or a green vegetable, such as spinach steamed until it barely wilts. Carol recommends beer, a Japanese brand if possible, or sake, as the best liquid accompaniments, although a white wine will do. Green tea traditionally ends the meal on a placid note—"except when people put sugar in it, which really horrifies me."

lawrence and carolyn noveck

Lawrence and Carolyn Noveck, much to their surprise, at present find themselves in the full bloom of a second career. Both had led long and active professional and business lives. As designer Carolyn Schnurer, Mrs. Noveck revolutionized bathing suit fashions; today she still spends hours in an office as the vice-president of an executive-search firm—"I could retire but I'd be bored to death in a geriatric atmosphere." Mr. Noveck was a successful manufacturer who decided to liquidate his company ten years ago. They consider themselves newlyweds—"We've only been married eight years"—and work at cultivating shared interests.

That food and entertaining are at the top of their list explains the Novecks' sudden triumphant and unexpected success as professional caterers. Such is the demand for their services that they now have to turn away almost 75 percent of the people who approach them. They themselves prepare every morsel of food to be served; at a large buffet this may mean cooking as many as thirty-five separate offerings. They practice ("We can't afford failures") and experiment ("We do unconventional things just for the sake of it") ahead of time. Their menus borrow from any cuisine that strikes their fancy—French, Italian, Chinese, Mexican, Polish—which they are likely to have mastered at one of the many cooking classes they continue to take. "Before we were married," Larry confesses, I'd never cooked. Now I'm hooked on it. The trouble is, there're never enough hours in the day for me." To save time, the Noveck's enroll separately in different types of classes and teach each other their newly acquired skills when they return to their own kitchen at night.

preferences

When entertaining in their Fifth Avenue duplex, which they like to do at least once a week no matter how busy they are, the Novecks like intimate dinners for 6 to 8, and big cocktail parties for 50 to 75. (For large-scale professional cooking, they've established a kitchen elsewhere.)

The Novecks, who always "case" a house before a catered party in order to study a client's space and equipment, are frequently dumbfounded by what they *don't* find. To entertain well, they insist, one must be properly equipped (for basic suggestions see page 57). And tidily organized. Before they actually start to cook a dish they measure out into bowls and little custard cups each and every ingredient listed in the recipe, which Larry will previously have typed step by step on a large index card which is shielded from kitchen stains in a clear plastic sheath and stored in a file. He will also have drawn up a daily calendar for the week or two preceding a party, depending on the relative elaborateness of its preparations. Shopping, cooking and freezing schedules are carefully plotted and faithfully followed. Special kitchen and service equipment will be checked. Conflicting demands for last-minute oven and burner space will be resolved. Aside from the usual *batterie de cuisine* the Novecks recommend a variety of helpful items for entertaining efficiently. These include: Oven, deep fat, candy and freezer thermometers; hot trays; electric skillet, deep fryer and handbeater; pastry tubes and bags; chopsticks for stirring and lifting; serrated knives; Chinese cleavers, including "a parsley cleaver which we use all the time—it's better balanced than a French knife;" a "mandoline" for slicing vegetables to a uniform thinness; a separate mill for white peppercorns; plenty of lidded plastic containers for prepared foods and storage; individual plastic ice-cube molds for freezing egg whites—"Date them, and you can keep them up to six months"; cheap aluminum disposable trays and roasting pans—"very desirable." The Novecks collect antique silver and marvelous copper cooking vessels which can be put on a buffet. For passing hot hors d'oeuvres, they find their silver ovenproof skillets with screw-in wooden handles indispensable. Gratinée pans "make wonderful a presentation of things like stuffed crêpes" (page 179). Crêpes, sometimes in batches of 350 to 400, are made in two well-seasoned pans; to season a crêpe pan, "fill with Mazola as close as possible to the brim. Heat slowly till very warm. Turn off and leave for 2-4 hours. Pour Mazola out and wipe pans with paper towels—never use water to clean. This way you can make crêpes as thin as tissue paper—you can freeze them in packages of 12, 16, 24 between squares of waxed paper. Then you wrap the stack tightly in foil."

food and drink

When the Novecks entertain at their own home, "we always have enough hors d'oeuvres to keep people comfortable while they're drinking." For a cocktail party they might have the following passed:

> Eggplant beignets (page 176)
> Cherry tomatoes, cubes of mozzarella and an-
>   chovies broiled briefly (2 to 3 minutes) on picks
> Croustades—small toasted bread cups—filled with
>   a coarse purée of mushrooms
> Miniature frankfurters in caraway-flecked pastry
>   blankets
> Squares of Greek spinach pie
> Chunks of steak or chicken in bourbon sauce
> Steak tartare balls rolled in chopped roasted
>   walnuts
> Hawaiian shrimp with soy
> Crudités

If more substantial buffet food is to follow, two hors d'oeuvres from this selection will be sufficient. For a cocktail buffet, the Novecks might serve sliced shell steaks on rounds of Italian bread, which can be eaten with the fingers, like open-faced sandwiches, or one of a variety of dishes which require a fork only—a *navarin* of lamb, a seafood casserole, chili with both chopped and cubed beef, bite-sized veal marengo, or "*leczo,*" a baked Hungarian discovery combining sliced sausages and vegetables and served with sour cream. These will be accompanied by salad and followed by a mouth-watering display of desserts, Larry's specialty—chocolate charlotte with a sauce of softened coffee ice cream, glazed fruits, baklava, lemon ice in lemon shells, a chocolate cream roll, orange compote in Grand Marnier. The meal always concludes with the Novecks' own blend of 13 ounces of light Medalin coffee to 3 ounces of dark.

When entertaining at small dinners, a typical menu, preceded by an hors d'oeuvre of eggplant beignets, might include:

> Cold Senegalese soup
> A casserole of chicken, white onions, potatoes

and baby artichokes

Endive and avocado salad

Fruit tart—an oblong of puff pastry patterned with
alternating sections of blueberries and seedless grapes

In this instance, cups of soup will be ready waiting on the table when the guests enter
the small oval dining room. However, the Novecks often prefer to serve a first course on
small plates in the living room, perhaps rolled smoked salmon stuffed with caviar and
whipped cream, or crêpes filled with mortadella, prosciutto, parmesan and ricotta (page
180). The used plates and forks will be swiftly stacked in the dishwasher, as the main
course is always served buffet style in the kitchen—"People love it, they think it's great
fun." (For quick clearing up, the Novecks remind us that pots and pans dry quickly when
whisked out of sight into a gas oven with a pilot light.)

geoffrey holder

Enter Geoffrey Holder, the Compleat Trinidadian, award-winning director and costume designer (The Wiz, etc.), choreographer, painter, dancer, singer, actor, author, photographer, mad raconteur and inspired cook. Although he is married to the hauntingly beautiful dancer and actress Carmen de Lavallade, their hectic professional schedules rarely permit the Holders to entertain together. However, with his stage director's ability to keep excitement mounting and his choreographer's flair for group movement, Geoffrey manages to single-handedly cope as cook, bartender, master of ceremonies and life of his own frequent parties, which can be given, it seems, at the drop of one of his many vast and rakish hats.

preferences

Geoffrey likes buffet dinners for twelve, after-theater gatherings, first-class rum, exotic, spice-sparked Caribbean food, friends who can play the piano or sing, and feet-up summer stag parties. On the other hand he avoids convenience foods, and abhors parties where everybody is obliged to stand.

111

atmosphere

The Holder ideal? "I like salons," he booms. "The key to a good party is choreographing the guests—one cab driver, one lawyer, one doctor, two actors for a little drama, three singers for Gregorian chants, and an occasional ex-president. The thing is to stay out of the way of your guests. I let them play musical chairs and find out what they have in common besides me. Let them find out what I saw in them."

Guests are invited by telephone for eight o'clock, never earlier, which gives them enough leeway "to tuck the children in, if they have any, or just refresh themselves. It gives the ladies a little time to relax and fluff up. Dress is understood to be casual chic. That means no ties for men and ladies in long nothings."

Once the guests arrive for dinner, and occasionally they may number as many as twenty, they'll find no trouble playing their host's version of social musical chairs. The apartment, painted dazzling white, is splendidly equipped with flexible seating arrangements. Not only are there studio couches and plenty of easily regroupable chairs, stools and cushions, but from under a round white Japanese coffee table, which can be adjusted to dining height, appear four wedge-shaped upholstered benches. In addition, sleek white chests run without interruption down the side walls of the long living room. These double as storage units and gallery display counters for the spectacular Holder collection of sculpture, art objects, giant plants and decoratively perched friends. Walls and furniture are starkly white, he explains, "so the people become accessories, the only color. You get great silhouettes against all the white—Negro lips, Jewish noses, dancers' necks—I mean the whole thing. I like to look at people beside statues of Mexican saints and African masks, through enormous palms and lots of lilies. People bring the statues to life. I always start off with bright lights at the beginning of the evening, but after dinner I dim down to candlelight to rest the eyes. Also, you don't see the ladies' make-up falling apart." By then, what with the jungles of greens and looming statuary, "everyone ends up looking like Dorothy Lamour."

During the hot months, Geoffrey likes to entertain summer bachelors whose wives are out in the Hamptons with the children. "I call it 'Holder's Home for Wayward Saints.' The main course is rum. With bitter lemon. Once I made them all put on togas. There's something relaxing about going to someone's house where you can shed. Like the Japanese taking their shoes off before entering the house. It makes you feel you're at home. That evening we sang impromptu Gregorian chants of Clive Barnes' *New York Times* reviews."

112

Never fussy about balanced numbers, Geoffrey might invite "a whole roomful of men and only three women, who will shine gloriously. Or, on the contrary, I might invite so many women that the apartment becomes a birdcage, with just three or four men to anchor it." In either case, self-service is the order of the day when food appears. Here, the Holder background scheme is carried over into plates and serving dishes of heavy white china, which set off the vivid tropical specialties of the house to perfection. Bought several dozen at a time, these are stashed away to replace inevitable breakage with a minimum of traipsing to and from the store. Aside from the food, the only blaze of color on the buffet is provided by candles in tall glass holders, and a fan-shaped stack of linen napkins in various shades of brilliant blues, greens, reds and oranges. This unexpected touch serves a practical purpose, for as Geoffrey points out, "There is always method in my madness. This way, guests can identify their napkins when they misplace them." There is method too in serving drinks in gigantic goblets, which may or may not match—"I can serve two drinks at once—it saves time and effort, it saves two trips! I believe in serving my own drinks, I believe it's part of my job. But I only serve the first round, then the gentlemen serve the ladies—it's a marvelous entrée into conversation. People forget that some men are shy and that they all want the right kind of introduction. Taking care of a lady's empty glass is a perfect solution."

food and drink

"For the first half-hour, I serve just drinks, never hors d'oeuvres or prissy little things that ruin the dinner. I like to turn people on to rum. Scotch is boring. Gin and tonic is a cop-out. Rum and bitter lemon is delicious and refreshing, a powerful, exotic flavor which combines marvelously with the powerful exotic flavors of my food. I've always got jugs of Almadén Chablis for anyone who wants it, and for non-drinkers I make my friend Charles Bowden's "Special"—club soda with a kick of Angostura bitters. But usually it's rum to begin with, and rum all the way through dinner. By the time dinner's through, nobody wants coffee. We just stay on with rum."

Geoffrey is justifiably acclaimed for his "Snake Bite" rum punch (page 206), which he recalls once "turned Lena Horne on and made her really sparkle."

Menus vary from the simple to the elaborate, depending on the mood, the weather or the occasion, but whatever the final dish, it will be sure to send off the heady aromas of traditional Caribbean cuisine, a potent compound of East Indian, Chinese, African,

113

Spanish and French cooking. For the summer bachelors, "a lot of red beans and meats" will fill the bill, but for a buffet dinner a much more varied and ambitious series of courses will be "strung out" one by one, the hot dishes being kept warm as they appear in shifts on an electric heating cart. Here is a typical Geoffrey Holder feast:

Bulljoul (a seafood and avocado salad; page 189)
Roast capon (boned by the butcher and stuffed
    by Mr. Holder with pork sausage, rosemary,
    garlic and scallions)
Yams (boiled and mashed with butter and "some
    chopped scallions for some texture")
Green beans sautéed in curry
A "green, white and red—my colors" salad of
    lettuce and cress, tomatoes and onion rings
    dressed with oil and vinegar

"I cook for people because I love them," he beams. This requires advance thought. Everything that needs chopping, cutting or slicing gets taken care of the night before. "People who are on a schedule like mine simply have to do that kind of tiresome thing ahead of time. I've got just one hour in that kitchen the night of the party." Carving while guests stand around clutching empty plates he thinks is a major time-consuming mistake that can destroy the tempo of a party. Accordingly he prefers easily served dishes such as hearty salads, whole baked fish, completely boned birds and beasts.

Following dinner, music keeps the party tempo from slackening. "A piano," says Geoffrey, "even the smallest one, keeps a party together. It keeps a home together. It used to be that after dinner people all sang together around the pianola. Extremely good, very good for the digestion."

Not even a business discussion can mar a Holder party mood. "I often ask business people with friends. Let's face it—you get to the point quickly. After the others have left, they can stay and chat and discuss whatever it is we have to talk out. I think the best time to discuss business is early in the morning. You think more clearly, and there's no distractions. And if you really want to end the whole thing right, you can just sit there and listen to Mabel Mercer."

stuart and carolyn levin

Carolyn and Stuart Levin thrive on entertaining, whether they're masterminding a ninety-nine-cannon extravaganza friends have asked them to manage, giving a four-star cocktail-buffet at their chic New York apartment, or serving up a simple summer lunch in the kitchen of their peaceful log cabin in the country. Both are well known in their respective fields; he is an imaginative restauranteur, as Carolyn Nesbitt she is a decorator and designer of textiles, wallpapers and carpets. Together, for the pleasure of sheer invention, they love to create fantastic party schemes for free-spending friends who turn to them for advice.

preferences

Devising "fantasies—always with a theme"—for 250 to 500 guests; seated dinners; cocktail buffets with music; small informal lunches in the country.

atmosphere

At what point does a social gathering stop being "a party" and become a "special event"? When it is conceived by the Levins. They evoke the ancient tradition of the banquet-festival, harking back to the days of the Roman Apicius, when a turbot garnished with swallow tongues might cost the price of ten slaves, or in the next millennium, the feasts of Duke Philip the Good of Burgundy, whose dinner décor once included a live Paris and three "goddesses" competing for an apple, a sixty-foot whale spouting sea gods and sirens, and a twenty-eight piece orchestra tootling beneath an edible pie crust.

A more recent Roman bacchanal was the party dreamed up by the Levins for a friend in Montego Bay. The theme was inspired by a collection of nude classical statues flanking the host's swimming pool. Invitations were sent forth from Philadelphia in the form of Latin proclamations calling on guests from all parts of the world to appear at the hostess' Jamaica residence wearing classical costume. At the appointed hour, the arrival of each was heralded by fanfares of trumpets. The octagonal living room was sheathed in a 360°

mural representing the Roman Forum and Coliseum fused into one. The faces of the guests, photographically superimposed onto figures in the arena's mob, stared down from the walls at a teeming scene of gold-tasseled, mauve, magenta and purple moiré splendor. Heavily draped tables were covered with whole lobsters and squab. The hostess was wheeled about on a decorated service cart. A professional spectacle was provided by fire eaters, magicians and a midnight eruption of skyrockets and catherine

116

wheels. The Levins ("that evening took absolutely everything out of us") by dawn were too tired to wait for the judgment of thumbs. "Thank God we left before we had to take it all down."

On a somewhat more mundane level, Stuart and Carolyn recall their recent "Fun City" party given to celebrate the streets of New York. Above each table's centerpiece bobbed a helium-filled balloon, snared in nylon mesh net and bearing a street name. Upon arrival each guest was given a parking ticket with a table "address" printed on it. Bicycle license plates stamped with first names were the place cards. Miniature mailboxes, spotted in the window of a gift shop in Morristown, New Jersey, were transformed into cigarette boxes. As Carolyn says, "If you keep on the lookout, you can find all kinds of crazy things to make a party special. People are really big children—they love to take favors home with them."

When entertaining their own friends, the Levins take a less flamboyant stance. In their apartment overlooking Central Park, with its living room upholstered in soft camel beiges and stunning persimmon red, Oriental blue and pearl-gray carpet, one of Carolyn's own designs, they like to give dinners, cocktail buffets, and after-performance suppers in honor of friends in the theater. The dining room, papered in shimmering silver on silver, is dominated by a stainless-steel and blue-lacquer table frequently massed "with the largest collection of Baccarat crystal animals outside the Baccarat showroom." Menus may focus on any style of cooking from French *haute cuisine* to Szechuan.

The Levins are both consummate cooks. For their country log cabin, Carolyn has designed a kitchen so that the two can work comfortably beside each other. "In the country we play menus by ear. We take a look around the local supermarket and forage in our garden." Carolyn preserves all her own tomato juice and jams. "We keep it simple. We found some terrific trays like shallow boxes. After they've been set you can stack one on top of the other without disturbing the plates and cutlery on the ones below. We serve summer lunches buffet style in the kitchen—crudités, cheeses, chicken in tarragon, vanilla ice cream with our own wild strawberries, wine—and people can either stay in the house or take their trays out under the trees, where we've spread out blankets and cloths. We always make a point of inviting our friends' children—it's important for them to feel included and for our own to have companions. And singles—you have to look out for your single friends and take care of them, particularly on holidays when they may feel lonely and neglected—even if it's only a half day in the country, it can make all the difference. The secret is for you yourself to relax and have a good time. If you make everything a production, it ceases to be fun. A party shouldn't be just an eating festival. Certainly the food should be good, but isn't it always secondary to the joy of good company?"

helen mc cully

Helen McCully, one of the country's most respected food authorities, champions contemporary efficiency and worthy old traditions with happy impartiality. Miss McCully is the food editor of *House Beautiful* and author of several popular books, among them, *Cooking with Helen McCully Beside You* and *Nobody Ever Tells You These Things About Food and Drink*. In keeping with the times, she has just published a practical volume entitled *Waste Not, Want Not*.

preferences

Small dinners for 4 to 6, seated buffets for 8, 9 or 10, and cocktail buffets.

atmosphere

Helen McCully, brought up in Nova Scotia, lives in a sunny Manhattan apartment which, aside from its super-modern kitchen, could almost be viewed as a nineteenth-century American time capsule. Victorian furniture from home is polished to a high sheen, primitive paintings in fine gilt frames make the white walls mellow. The dining room is painted the rich autumnal blush of a maple leaf. Snowy antique china and lustrous silver gleam against dark wooden

sideboard and table: "I keep all the old things out—how can you enjoy them if you keep everything locked 'safely' away?" But there is no mustiness of a museum; this is an evocation of a past in which vital people can live.

Lin Yutang once wrote that patriotism is all the good things one ate in one's childhood. Helen's approach to food is at once experimental and nostalgic. Culinary expertise has apparently come naturally: "We were always very interested in what we ate. I was born and grew up (as did my mother before me) in the big and lovely old Victorian house built by my Grandfather Lowerison. Mother loved to cook and garden, but Susan, who came to my grandparents' at the age of twelve, did all the major cooking. 'A good plain cook,' Mother used to say.

"I think we had the original deep-freeze—a double-walled room built inside the carriage house was filled with hay, and it was in this room frozen birds (chickens, turkeys, ducks, geese) were buried against the day they were needed. The plucked birds, brought to us by several farmers, were tied compactly and hung around the walls of the woodhouse (above cat and dog level) to freeze. In November in Nova Scotia you could depend on the weather being cold enough to do the freezing for you. Once frozen, the birds were wrapped in newspapers (printer's ink is a deterrent to rodents) with cayenne pepper—also a rodent deterrent—between the layers, tied securely, then buried in the hay. When Susan wanted a couple of chickens or a turkey she'd send our man to the 'freezer.' The birds were, of course, thawed to cook. Curiously, I thought everybody lived the way we did. Following my grandfather's pattern we also fattened a couple of pigs every year. So, we had our own hams and learned to love head cheese. In the fall, my father would order a barrel of oysters, which were put in the cold room in the cellar, and any child who felt like an oyster could take an oyster knife and go down and eat his fill.

"Christmas was the most marvelous time for us. One year, my brother, sister and I went downstairs after Santa Claus had left and found a real live pony standing in the big room. Fires were burning in both fireplaces, the Christmas tree was bright with real candles, and our stockings, stuffed with goodies, hung from one of the mantels."

From a letter her mother wrote to a favorite aunt years ago, Helen gave us the following menu served one Christmas:

Oyster Cocktails
Bouillon
Shrimp and mushroom rosettes
Roast stuffed turkey

Cranberries
Peas   Puréed potatoes
Baked ham
Rum punch*
Plum pudding with brandy sauce
Frozen pudding with claret sauce and whipped
   cream
Nuts   Raisins
Candies   Grapes
Bonbons
Coffee

Decorating for Christmas was a cherished rite, Mrs. McCully reported to her sister: "As I made myself 18 wreaths and Vena (the housemaid) tied me several yards of spruce. The casement on the doors I draped or outlined with the greening, finishing with the bells. The windows were done the same way. The mantle I banked with holly with a couple of lovely velvet poinsettias stuck in artistically. On each wreath I put a poinsettia at different angles and hung them around the room with three on the window curtains. I covered a wire frame for my lamp shade and hung tiny bells all around it and twined holly around the edge. On the plate rail I placed red candles at regular intervals all around the room. Had one or two sprays of holly alternating with the wreaths with a poinsettia stuck somewheres. Herb [Helen's father] sent me up three lovely primroses and a beautiful azalea which I had arranged in different spots. Red candles on the mantle, sideboard and dinner table. You can imagine how delighted I was when your lovely baskets came in. The large one I used for a centre piece with a pot of ferns and white hyacinths in it. It was lovely under the red shade. I had that long runner Nell Ryan [an old friend living in Paris] gave me and I placed candles on the extreme ends of it with the small baskets half way between them in the centre."

Helen says, "I usually give a Christmas cocktail buffet, which my foreign students love. About eight or nine years ago I met a young French graduate student who'd been in America for two years and was about to return home for good. I was horrified when he told me he'd never been invited into an American private home. Not once. Well, that started it. Now it's like having a new family. Each year I get one or two new arrivals

---

* "'Which,' Mother added, 'Mrs. McCully licked up in fine style.' This was my father's mother, a Baptist, which mother (Church of England) thought was the absolute end. As perhaps you know, a good Baptist doesn't drink or play cards—both of which my mother did and enjoyed thoroughly."

through the Institute of International Education, an organization that brings over graduate and exchange students. You start with one and build up a great loving relationship, and then it just grows. Now I always have at least four or five from all over the world. My house becomes their home. They can bring their girl friends, their boy friends. They want to know if I approve. We discuss their problems, their secrets, their ambitions. When I have parties I ask them all. They all help—mixing drinks, pouring wine, serving. They add zest and life to a party—it's immediately more cosmopolitan, more fun. Why else would you give a party? I want people to have a good time."

What makes for a good party? "People must circulate. I hate men who stand talking to each other. I don't mean I'm running around bossing everybody, but I'll say, 'You've been talking to each other long enough, now go talk to so and so.' That goes for young couples in love, too. Coming unglued for a couple of hours isn't going to kill them. In fact it might be good for them—you know what I mean: fan the flames."

On other subjects as well, Helen is a mine of saltily expressed personal opinions. On the need for an interesting guest list: "Look, if you have a lot of dumb people, you're going to have a dumb party." On social mores: "I'm annoyed by bad manners. People who pick up the bottle to look at the label or turn a plate over to look at the hallmark. Putting cigarettes out in wine coasters, which has happened to me. People who don't call or write to say thank you." On social realities: "Putting on the dog when you have no servants is absolutely ridiculous."

food

And on her specialty, cooking: "You have to be courageous and accept the fact that everybody has failures. Nobody's *that* great. If everything's a success, you learn nothing, although if you keep your eyes open you can learn something every time you pick up a spoon."

Today at Christmastime, Helen serves the following elegantly understated cocktail buffet:

Chicken liver pâté (page 175)
Baked ham with apricot glaze (page 194)

Dijon mustard
Raw mushrooms with sauce rémoulade
Brie
French bread

For those who "hang on" she always has a sweet (baklava or brownies) and good coffee.

barbara d'arcy

Barbara D'Arcy, Bloomingdale's presiding genius of store design, is noted internationally for her unerring instinct for recognizing, well before others, new visual moods and trends in their embryonic stage. Bursting with talent, energy and unquenchable good cheer, she and her husband, furniture designer Kirk White, love to travel, shop, garden, cook and decorate—enthusiasms which make them ideal candidates for creative entertaining.

preferences

In their city apartment, devoid of a dining room, dinners for 6 to 8 and cocktail parties for as many as 75. In the country, seated dinners for 6 to 8 or outdoor buffet lunches, with tables set up on the lawn, for up to 125.

atmosphere

Obviously, the author of *The Bloomingdale Book of Home Decoration* holds strong opinions on the subject of her surroundings. Probably more than any other designer, Ms. D'Arcy was instrumental in popularizing the "eclectic look." As to decorating for parties, she recalls, "I was part of the whole farm-table movement, what you might call 'the peasantry approach.' Before we got started, people had been so cautious, they never would have dared to mix all those different elements together—bare wooden tables, brass, pewter, pottery, glass, antique and modern objects. It got to the point where I was even putting fine old silver and clay flower pots together. I guess it started in the fifties; the world was just beginning to open up in those days, people began to travel, to expose themselves to new cultures. First they went to France, Spain, Italy and England, later to the Near and Far East and South America. It was wonderful. I'd be gone on Bloomingdale's buying sprees for two or three months at a time and come home positively laden with bundles. In those days you could still find real treasures, all the goodies. I built up a backlog of literally hundreds of pieces of memorabilia. I used to open my closet, look in and say, 'How am I going to put it together today?'

"Color was everything. I wouldn't have been caught dead with white napkins. Even the glassware was usually colored. One of my favorite combinations was a white service plate banded in gold and orange beneath small, Spode ones patterned in blues and orange and white. I'd set these on a beautifully battered sixteenth-century worktable, along with orange napkins and orange goblets. Down the center of the table I might have laid a silk runner or a length of antique ribbon. Then, for added interest, mixed bits and pieces of antique and modern porcelain. Vegetables we'd serve in pottery bowls, meat on wooden boards. And clusters, I'm still very big on clusters. My father-in-law gave us a superb collection of Indian baskets. I'd cluster five or six in all sizes and fill them with spring flowers or different breads, rolls and breadsticks.

"Now, almost overnight, I'm beginning to change. It was a case of sudden inspiration. Recently we were invited to the prettiest dinner party we'd been to in years. It just hit me between the eyes. It was so old-world beautiful, so classic, elegant, romantic. And fun! The table was covered to the floor in a crisp, beautifully pressed white organdy cloth. White and gold and silver and crystal all gleaming magnificently in the candlelight. Gloppy gold and white service plates, low white flowers, perfectly polished silver, Baccarat candlesticks. We sat in needlepoint chairs embroidered by the hostess. It really took you back in time. But nothing stuffy about it—these were dynamic, very up people. They had all the latest Hustle music playing gently in the background. After we left, my husband turned to me and announced, 'No more wood.' We'd had blackened old silver stashed away for years. Suddenly we couldn't wait to get it all out. Having shunned it for so long, I now crave silver serving dishes, platters, candlesticks—prettiness, yes, I'll say it, *graciousness* and femininity."

Barbara points out that classic tableware and accessories are a perfect foil for the new uncluttered look of many avant-garde interiors. Her own apartment has recently been stripped of all excessive décor: "Now you can actually see the tops of tables. We've declared a moratorium on buying small things. Of course we both violate the rules. Like the eight smaller-than-small Chinese bowls, perfect for melted butter for artichokes, that of course, I was unable to resist. However, the brass candlesticks, the pewter, the pottery, the wooden plates, the colored glassware, and all the other rustic stuff has been carted to the country. Even still, the pendulum never swings completely back. What I want to do is bring eclecticism back to formality."

How does Barbara plan to bring off this interesting marriage? "Now I'd love to have beautiful Madeira or snowy organdy cloths. I'll set up a round table and cover it to the floor. I'll use the same orange-and-gold-banded service plates, but with clear crystal rather than busily patterned smaller dishes. Instead of the orange stemware, I'll use some fabulous goblets we had copied from ancient ones we found in the glass museum in Venice. Instead of orange napkins, white, off-white or old luncheon-sized écru linen ones with a lace border. And all my mother's silver. And maybe one or two interesting antique accessories. I'd never abandon variety. It adds spice to life. I'd never want to own a whole matched set of china with all the serving dishes."

"Remember," Barbara cautions, "that I'm talking about classic, citified elegance, not the relaxed country life. As far as total eclecticism is concerned, in the country there's no other way out. For a small weekend dinner I love a scheme of greens, cream Wedgwood, pewter and wooden plates, giant shells for salad or fruit, red pottery from the south of France. For big outdoor buffet lunches, we cover card tables either in three shades of yellow, orange and shocking pink or in a blue-and-white flame-stitch pattern. When you invite 125 people for lunch, believe me, you'll have to mix *everything*."

food and drink

Barbara concentrates on food which is "rarely complex, but looks pretty and tastes good. A humble hearty soup becomes a thing of beauty in a wonderful old tureen. If you can put a simple, delicious meal together, can open a wine bottle and have a flair for presentation, you've got it made."

luisa-esther and patrick flynn

Luisa-Esther Flynn, the vibrant Argentinian wife of New Yorker E. Patrick Flynn, is a hostess of great stamina and skill. They entertain often at their Manhattan town house, their farm in Carmel, or at the Southampton shores. That they share interests in many fields is quickly discerned at any one of their many parties, where the worlds of international business, politics and the arts are made to connect rather than collide.

preferences

Seated dinners for 4 to 24 and informal Argentine barbecues. "I prefer smaller parties to big ones," Luisa-Esther explains. "Big parties are a problem in a town house or at a resort because of ... you couldn't describe them exactly as crashers ... because of people who get themselves brought along by someone they know's been invited. It can really get out of control. You look around and say, my God! Who are they? Where am I? Anyway, it's much more interesting to be able to talk to people without being interrupted every ten seconds to meet somebody whose name you can't even hear. And I refuse to use people. I don't want to tell you how many times I've been seated next to the one person who doesn't understand English because the hosts know I speak several languages—you're immediately off on a desert island with this person, whether you like him or not. Also, if you've asked someone as an extra woman or man, it's only fair to tell them so in advance. And I can't bear pretension—like people who have some second-rate caterer with tired food for a black-tie dinner in a small apartment—they think they're dressing the place up, but it's a disaster."

atmosphere

Before dinner, the Flynns' guests convene for drinks on the second floor in a striking Persian library bright with printed fabric walls and an open fire. When dinner is announced, they adjourn to a spectacular ground-floor dining room which looks out on a spotless whitewashed walled garden thickly blanketed in inky green ivy. The walls of the dining room, paved from ceiling to floor with mirror, reflect infinities of dancing candlelight. Two round tables permanently reside there; if one alone is in use, the other is skirted to the floor in dark silk and decked with a simple still life of objets d'art. The dining table wears a long crisp uniform of white organza over white linen. Antique silver and Meissen and Baccarat crystal are its decorative focal points. "If you have beautiful place settings, then candles, wine carafes and maybe some grapes with pine cones are enough. And you should be able to see the people—they're the whole point."

food and drink

Although blessed with a resident Spanish cook and butler, Luisa-Esther not only plans the menus and shops but frequently cooks a major part of a meal. The menus for her dinner parties might most accurately be described as "classic continental." A typical meal might begin with a Spanish gazpacho (page 181) and proceed through an Italian main course and a French dessert.

Single-handedly, that is to say once Patrick's expertly laid charcoal fires have reached a desired degree of even, smoldering heat, she occasionally likes to introduce friends to a traditional Argentine barbecue, a no-nonsense feast to be consumed slowly over several hours. Children love these casual South American fiestas, as they can fly off and play between what one might more aptly call the "stages" rather than "courses" of the meal. There are no frills: "I came from a pioneering country," Luisa-Esther announces proudly, "where the food is very simple."

The specialness of an Argentine barbecue lies in the diversity of meats that are served; a standard menu:

An Argentine Barbecue

Italian sausages, both the hot and sweet varieties
Chorizos
Liver
Lamb chops
Kidneys
Sweetbreads
Short ribs of beef in one piece
A large marinated piece of beef
Argentinian Barbecue Sauce (page 196)
Baked potatoes
Salad of lettuce, onion and tomato
Fruit salad and homemade cookies
Red wine

Needless to say, one can cut down on the number of meats, but a certain variety should still be maintained. If anything, the Argentinians add rather than subtract; however, such native favorites as braided tripe may fall a little beyond the general North American ken.

Luisa-Esther describes how to orchestrate the event: "Don't put everything in at once. First grill the sausages for an appetizer to eat at the table with wine. You relax and have a nice conversation. Then you gradually put the small pieces on—the sweetbreads, the liver, small lamb chops and the others. We put salt and pepper on the meat first. The flame must never touch the meat—if grease falls on the charcoal you must sprinkle the flame with water immediately. Cook the meats very slowly. Put potatoes in the ashes to bake. Then you put the big piece of meat on—a large London broil for example—and let it cook while you're eating the small pieces. You can marinate the London broil overnight in red wine, olive oil, chopped shallots, salt, pepper and basil if you like. Talk some more, drink some more red wine. Soon the big piece will be done. In Argentina we like to make our own barbecue sauce (page 196) to season the meat at the table, not while it's cooking. With teen-agers you won't have to worry about having too much—you never know, you might not even have enough."

gary and naomi graffman

Gary Graffman, one of the United States' foremost concert pianists, and his witty wife Naomi spend much of their life on the professional wing. Whenever possible they pause in their world travels to entertain friends in their enormous-roomed old New York apartment, only a bouquet's throw from Carnegie Hall. Once a subject catches the Graffmans' interest—whether it be music, food, wine, ridiculous postcards or rare Southeast Asian porcelains—they pursue it with unflagging enthusiasm. Loyal and thoughtful friends, Naomi and Gary take particular pleasure in honoring musical colleagues at decidedly upbeat after-recital supper parties.

preferences

Small seated dinners for 6 to 8 prefaced by a sampling of Gary's specialties of the house. After-the-performance buffets for 25 to 50 guests: "Ned Rorem," Naomi informs us, "quite rightly defines a concert as 'that which precedes a party.' "

atmosphere

By-passing a vast living room crammed with two grand pianos, upholstered Victoriana and superb Oriental art, a dinner guest is led directly into a smaller room dominated by an imposing bar and an incredible collection of bottles. "It would be loathesome," Gary beams, "not to have a complete complement of alcoholic beverages with a bar this size." Like many of the Graffmans' possessions it has an interesting history; it is, in fact, a desanctified altar. The high, bentwood bar chairs once graced an old-fashioned soda fountain. "What flavor?" demands Gary, lining up a regiment of small Pakistani silver cups and frosty unlabeled pint bottles of seemingly identical clear liquids before the visitor's puzzled gaze. "Lemon? Tangerine? Grapefruit? Lime? Orange? Pepper?" The confusion deepens. "Or possibly buffalo grass?"

Gary Graffman's flavored vodkas are potent evidence of an unusual drink's power to make a party take off. He lays in an inexpensive house-brand vodka and then selects

flavoring agents at the fruit market, the spice rack, the Polish pharmacy. For a citrus-scented vodka, only a single piece of fruit is needed. With a sharp potato-peeler, remove the skin in strips, taking pains to avoid any bitter white pith. The strips of zest are then dropped into a quart bottle of vodka, which should remain at room temperature for about three days. Taste the brew after two days to see whether the flavor is sufficiently strong. If it is, the vodka should be filtered through a fine sieve, capped in pint bottles and stored in the freezer. The flavor of spicy Russian Pertzovka is reproduced by adding two teaspoons of equal parts of black, white and Jamaican peppercorns, cracked or coarsely ground, into a quart of vodka. The bottle should be shaken regularly, and the liquor strained into pint bottles after three days. The pungent "Zubrovka" is made by the same method, with a dozen or so strands of "buffalo" or "sour" grass, obtainable at some pharmacies or Polish and Ukranian markets. Akvavit calls for a teaspoon of caraway seeds, a pinch of fennel seeds and a sliver of bitter orange zest.

Naomi, an adventurous and talented cook, might fill little glasses of orange or lime vodka to drink with a tart *seviche* at the outset of this summertime dinner:

> Seviche of shrimp and bay scallops
> Cold roast pork stuffed with tongue
> Salad of apples, potatoes and scallions in a
>   homemade mayonnaise with basil and parsley
> Craig Claiborne's hazelnut cheesecake with
>   Naomi's bittersweet chocolate topping

Being almost constantly on tour, the kind of party with which the Graffmans by default have become most familiar is the after-concert supper in their honor. Naomi herself is a master at post-concert entertainments, but not following a Graffman recital—Gary cannot be expected to worry about the bar being properly set up while preparing himself mentally for the performance. Instead, the party will be for a chum—perhaps Eugene Istomin, Claude Frank or Leon Fleisher. The guests will include mutual friends as well as those specified on the guest of honor's list. Naomi prepares a prodigious fork supper for 25 to 50 ahead of time—"otherwise I would have hysterics."

Deep from her card catalogue she pulls a repertoire of dishes, ranging from Moroccan couscous with sweet meatballs to cutlets of minced chicken in sour cream and mustard sauce, that reheat brilliantly. A recent menu included:

> Guarneri salad (invented by Mrs. Graffman for a
>   party in honor of the quartet of that name;
>   page 183)
> Mrs. Artur Rubinstein's Polish bigos (adapted
>   somewhat by Mrs. G.; page 190)
> Crêpes stuffed with minced boiled beef and dill in
>   mushroom sauce
> Crêpes stuffed with spinach and cheese in cheese
>   sauce
> Ham cubes in Madeira sauce
> Green salad in small pieces
> Brie and bread
> Fruit and homemade cookies or brownies

carl jerome

Carl Jerome, director of the James Beard Cooking School, is a forthright young bachelor fired by a passion for his work. As a host, he strives to meld elegant aromas and tastes with relaxed simplicity.

preferences

Dinner parties, given at the customary hour or after a play or the opera, for never more than 6 guests. Friends are invited to work along with the host in his well-equipped kitchen, an exercise which allows them to participate in both the mysteries and rewards of culinary creation. Guests are expected to dress casually, to the point where they're asked to take off jackets and ties.

atmosphere

Carl's Greenwich Village kitchen has been installed in what was once a front bedroom looking down on a picturesque, tree-lined street. The room is divided into work and dining areas by a broad counter on which food is both prepared and served. His dining table is a gleaming old hatch cover, large enough to accommodate six or seven diners, set on sturdy legs in front of a working fireplace. The rest of the furniture is simple, in keeping with the two-room apartment's dominant tone of brisk, sensible efficiency. While there will be flowers, for example, they will never be set on the dining table—their fragrance might intrude upon that of the food. On occasion, however, a touch of the bizarre is introduced by the simultaneous functioning of fireplace and air conditioner. Why? "I love to toast bread for caviar over the flames."

Carl, who never serves more than three courses, including a cheese or dessert, rarely plans a menu more than two days in advance, one reason being that "it's important to see what the weather's like. Even in June it can be a ghastly day, so you don't want a cold soufflé or jellied soup." Soup, he insists, is best as a meal in itself. He cites as a recent example a seated supper for sixty-five in California, at which the menu consisted

solely of a robust minestrone with grated parmesan, bread, cheese, fruit, chocolate cake and wine. The hosts thoughtfully included this menu in the invitation "so that their guests would know that soup was *it* for the evening."

Carl skips hors d'oeuvres—"they can nibble on what they're preparing"—and he's come to the conclusion that it's best to dish up the guests' main course for them from the side; "otherwise their plates all look like hell on the table—too few people know how to properly block a runny sauce with food barriers."

A recent Jerome menu, with all hands at work, took a mere one hour and twenty minutes to prepare, including the shopping:

A Cook-Along Dinner

Hot artichokes with mustard mayonnaise
Rack of lamb persillé with sautéed potatoes
Pears poached in red wine and served with heavy
    cream

Once guests assembled, the schedule was this:

1)   Artichoke water put on to boil. Potatoes peeled and cut.

2)   Guests trim artichokes and drop them in boiling water.

3)   Meanwhile one person has started to pare the pears . . .

4)   While Carl trims the meat . . .

5)   Pears put to poach gently in red wine and sugar (depending on their firmness, pears can take up to 1½ hours to cook through).

6)   Fresh white bread crumbs prepared and parsley finely chopped. Potatoes sautéed.

7)   Then: As artichokes take 45 minutes and the rack of lamb 30 minutes to cook, the lamb is put into a 450° oven 30 minutes after the artichoke water has come to a boil—this allows 15 minutes in which to eat the artichokes (the mustard mayonnaise can be made in the blender or food processor in the batting of an eye). After 20 minutes in the oven, the lamb is removed and basted with 1½ cups of good red wine (left over from the pears); when good and wet, the lamb is given a thick coating of equal parts of thoroughly mixed parsley and crumbs. The broiler is turned on, and the lamb is run beneath it for 3 to 4 minutes or until the coating is nicely browned; it can then "rest" 6 to 8 minutes, uncovered,

before carving. Wine, rather than hard liquor, is consumed before and throughout the meal—an open bottle of Fils Jacques California Cabernet is left on the counter for guests to help themselves from while they work. Some people like whipped cream with the pears, but Carl prefers them plain. The meal concludes with espresso.

loredana and pierre van goethem

Loredana Van Goethem, the type of soft-spoken Northern Italian blonde who makes willows look stunted, is the Venetian wife of a Belgian economist and financier. They make their home in Manhattan, where they regularly entertain wave upon wave of friends from many lands.

preferences

Seated buffet dinners for 16 to 30 guests, the table arrayed with a colorful profusion of Italian dishes. A gigantic annual cocktail party for up to 300 people: "To catch everyone you haven't seen. You can ask *anybody* to a big cocktail, except maybe Al Capone or someone who smokes marijuana and the police come."

atmosphere

Loredana's years of professional experience in the world of European high fashion have trained her to decorate with an eye toward sleek elegance and tightly coordinated color. The large living room and adjacent dining room is a surpassing exercise in blue-and-white pattern on pattern, silver on chrome, crystal on glass, with an occasional complementary flash of persimmon or robin's-breast red. The theme is carried into party décor: at small dinners, the long contemporary glass table is set with glass candlesticks and small blue and red Chinese vases filled with daisies. For seated buffet parties, two or three large collapsible round tables are covered to the floor in blue; china is blue and white, as are the African batik napkins. At each place lies a little bundle of Italian bread sticks tied with red ribbon. The buffet table will be decorated with a mound of fresh fruit (a tall pyramid of red apples at Christmastime) and, of course, a sumptuous display of Loredana's native cuisine.

139

food and drink

In matters of food, Loredana has developed a most intriguing philosophy—she claims that it is much less drudgery to make many different dishes in easy-to-manage portions than a few in vast quantities: "It defeats me, all these heavy pots, all this chopping of only one thing, all this physical struggle. With many dishes you can give a more amusing menu, more varied—people choose what they like or try a little of everything. It makes it more an occasion." What does this entail? "Oh, one red pasta, one white pasta, a rice dish, an egg dish, many salads, many vegetables, two or even three main courses, some cheeses, some desserts . . ." Very well. One may save oneself from muscular exhaustion, but what about a nervous breakdown? "It is really very easy. You make everything before."

Upon reflection, her view seems right. Baked pasta and rice dishes nowadays are far too frequently overlooked when planning a buffet menu. Their virtues are many—they are delicious, easy to serve, easy to eat, and can be prepared a day in advance. Italian *frittatas,* in which sautéed vegetables are bound together with beaten eggs to form a kind of parmesan-glazed omelet, can be cooked hours in advance and served in pizza-like wedges at room temperature. Cooked vegetable salads, either marinated or dressed in mayonnaise, can also be prepared at one's leisure ahead of time (without mayonnaise, up to three days); a dusting of freshly chopped parsley or other herbs at the last minute snaps them instantly back to life. Green beans (Loredana likes frozen Italian-style broad beans) in fresh tomato sauce can withstand a gentle reheating, as can vegetable purées. The beans and tomatoes can also be served cold as a salad. For the meat course, Loredana deep-fries breaded veal cutlets *alla Milanese* until crisply crusted; these can sit for several hours until served at room temperature. As a hot dish, she browns, then braises an eye round of beef with coarsely chopped onion, carrot, shallots, parsley, celery, red wine and a big bouquet garni until fork tender. The beef is sliced, arranged in an ovenproof dish and moistened with a sauce of the vegetables puréed in the blender with the skimmed pan juices. Before serving, the dish is reheated slowly. Mixed salad greens are washed and kept on the ready in plastic bags in the refrigerator. Cheeses are unwrapped and left for several hours to come to flavorful room temperature. Desserts (which are served at the tables or set out on the buffet, once all the other dishes have been cleared away) are either simple homemade ones—strawberry shortcake, for example, chocolate mousse, or blueberries and ice cream, or bought: "Sometimes it's true, you can't do absolutely everything."

Here is a sample Loredana menu for a memorable

Italian Buffet Dinner

Baked pasta Siciliana (designated "red pasta," as
    is any pasta dish in which there is a prevalence
    of tomatoes in the sauce)
Baked pasta shells, macaroni or *"penne"* ("pens")
    in béchamel (a "white pasta" in that it is bound
    with cream sauce; page 186)
Sartú of rice (page 187)
Frittata of zucchini
Green beans in tomato sauce
Hearts of palm and tomato vinaigrette
Cotoletta alla Milanese (deep fried veal cutlets)

Brasata (braised eye round of beef)

Endive, watercress and raw mushroom salad in oil
and lemon dressing

Cheese board with Swedish flatbread, plain
crackers and breadsticks with sesame seed

Chocolate mousse, strawberry shortcake or blueberries with ice cream

Neapolitan espresso or Sanka or a *tisane,* a soporific infusion of mint or rose hips

Note: Bottles of both red and white wine are put
on tables.

whitney warren

Whitney Warren is a breezily competent young New Yorker who pursues a dauntingly busy career as a professional party consultant. Her expert advice is sought both by charitable organizations and private clients when they find themselves faced with the dilemma of entertaining large groups. But "coping with the masses" never fazes her—Whitney can and has handled literally a thousand people at a time.

preferences

"I believe in nothing forced or unnatural, nothing overly formal," whether it concerns a vast cocktail reception, a dinner dance, a lawn party or charity ball. "When dealing with large numbers, one has to rely on common sense—you've got to be frank about your space limitations and either remedy the situation or adjust to it by cutting back on your list. Try to think everything out beforehand—the best way I know how, although it may sound a little discouraging, is to always prepare for the worst."

What should be one's first consideration when entertaining a very large group—at a wedding, for example, or some community function where the guest list may include 100 to 500 people? "Getting them in and getting them out! Seriously, traffic is always the biggest problem, starting from the moment guests pull up in their cars. Professional parkers can tell you how many cars can be taken care of realistically—and it's also a good idea to advise the local police that you're expecting a traffic problem. Once in the house, it becomes a question of physical comfort and mobility. No one should be too cold, too hot, too wet or too crowded. It's the physical things that can put you off.

"A garden party is always chancy unless there's sufficient shelter. Think about having a tent erected, if you're willing to pull out all the stops. You should be prepared for an unseasonably chilly day—even in June, I've had to have tents heated. All fabrics in tents *must* be flameproofed. If the weather's cold, butane heaters should be turned on for two hours before guests arrive. By the same token, you mustn't leave people to broil in the sun or suffocate in an un-air-conditioned room during a heat wave. Powerful fans can be a help."

What else can one do to make a large party flow? "As I say, mobility is terribly important. Cut-off rooms at the ends of a corridor are no good—you end up with a group of little isolated parties. Always remember that people want to see what's going on; they don't want to feel as if they'd been stuck away in a corner. Again, you might try to connect rooms by enclosing part of the great outdoors. To ease the flow, remove all ditsy pieces of furniture like footstools, but don't get too carried away—the cleared-out look can seem rather *desperate* in a private house."

What about décor? "At a very large party there's no need to go wild on flowers and food. The idea is to create a festive and natural setting. Light is important, of course. Flower arrangements should be kept above eye level, but not on huge stands or columns, which always look as if they've been imported expressly for the occasion. Anyway, floral stands send me the negative message of a funeral. Flowers are better placed more naturally on mantlepieces or in other visible spots such as on top of a highboy. I love chandeliers decorated with fronds, and Chinese urns filled with lovely tall sprays of apple blossom or quince which one can also see through.

"Pink bulbs are the best. Floor lighting is good in tents—it diminishes the cavernous look. Try spotlights recessed in deep cylinders. I love candlelight more than anything, but once my hair caught fire at a party from a low candle on a mantlepiece. You have to be extremely careful. Low votive lights are a wise idea for tables—no chance that way of a floating chiffon sleeve going up in flame. If you are going to use the regular kind, though, find out in advance how fast they'll burn, which will depend on how strong a draft there may be. Candles burn so quickly if there's a breeze, and a hostess can't run around changing them when they've melted down."

food and drink

The easiest solution, of course, is to hire a caterer. Whether this will be the case or not, Whitney advises that the menu and drinks be kept simple. If the meal is to be served seated, the first course should be awaiting the guests on the tables as they take their places. Something fairly substantial, such as a slice of pâté or terrine *en gelée* with baskets of bread, appeases hunger more satisfactorily than a thin soup (which perforce must be cold). If the meal is served buffet style, a more practical method, skip the first course and begin with a main one. Dishes should be chosen which are attractive and easy to serve—"If food *looks* good, you're off to a better start." They should not be a mess by the time half the platter has been dished up. Put carafes or bottles of wine right on the dining tables. If possible, have empty plates cleared away and the dessert served

at the tables to avoid making everyone rise again. Whitney suggests that an ideal buffet menu for large numbers might consist of:

Canneloni (with meat, cheese and béchamel sauce, but not tomatoes. Convenient because they are rolled in individual portions, which are easy and neat to serve. Also, large batches can be made in advance and reheated in the oven at the last moment)

Baked tomato halves with parslied bread crumbs (again, easy and neat)

Mixed salad (with the lettuce torn into small pieces)

Fresh strawberries in raspberry purée

or

Chinese chicken (cubed with vegetables, soy and fresh ginger)

Fried rice

Salad

Trifle

The host might also consider alternative ways to save on service, time and effort. For example, all food might be packed in individual picnic baskets ready for guests to take to their tables. Or, each table might be colorfully set with either one huge picnic basket or its own small buffet from which guests may help themselves. The bar should be stocked only with the basics—Scotch, bourbon, vodka, gin, dry vermouth, as well as white and red wine (even for cocktail parties) and either orange or tomato juice.

ruth and harvey spear

Ruth Spear is the compiler and author of *The East Hampton Cookbook,* an extremely helpful volume originally published by the Ladies Village Improvement Society to celebrate that constructive organization's eightieth anniversary. Mistress of a spacious and charmingly Anglophilic New York apartment, Ruth, wife of lawyer Harvey Spear and mother of two small children, spends summers and year-round weekends on the sandy stretches of the tip of Long Island. One would never guess from her dreamy smile, serene manner and unabashedly sensuous appreciation of good food that Ruth is in fact a formidable paragon of organizational ability. She turns these talents to solving the tiresome logistic problems which perpetually haunt anyone responsible for the care and feeding of that many-mouthed specter, the weekend guest.

preferences

Ruth actually enjoys coping with a full weekend's entertaining, as long as everything's been thought through and brought under control: "I like to cook, but I don't like daily demands." As guests sometimes bring their own children along, this can mean planning double menus into the bargain. In the country, of course, all entertaining is casual; in the city the same organizational skills are applied to large formal dinners and buffet parties.

atmosphere

In the country, whenever possible, meals are eaten out of doors. Although a permanent table stands on the terrace, Ruth prefers to set up a long collapsible one covered with a checked cloth on the lawn beneath spreading trees—"This fulfills a private fantasy I have about being transported spiritually to Italy. Also, there's nothing more restful after eating and drinking wine than sliding down into the grass." The table, if decorated at all, may display a basket of "eggplants, red peppers and cabbages from the garden, which absolutely overwhelm me with their beauty." Bright red bandannas are used for napkins. Sometimes the table is set up as a buffet; patchwork quilts are spread on the lawn for guests to loll over lunch. At dinner, the same scenes are illuminated by kerosene lamps;

through stereo speakers Elizabethan and Renaissance background music drifts melo-
diously on the night air.

food and drink

Ruth's principles of weekend organization can be adopted equally well by someone
expecting guests to spend a few days at a permanent home rather than an informal

vacation house. Plans take form in the city on Wednesday, when Ruth plots all the weekend menus, so that supplies can be ordered and delivered on Thursday. This is necessary in order that advance preparations can be accomplished on Friday morning, freeing the hostess from most weekend kitchen and shopping chores. Raw vegetables are trimmed, cheeses are wrapped, and fruit, berries and fresh eggs—"If you've got eggs, you're never bereft"—packed. Ruth then prepares two or three favorite "extenders" ("I don't like the word, but that's exactly what they are") as well as the main course for Friday night; these dishes keep particularly well and can be used to "extend any meal—with any leftovers they make a decent lunch, even if it's just a dab with a sandwich." Included among them are old-fashioned coleslaw, ratatouille, and a variety of interesting salads—Russian, French potato (simply dressed in olive oil and vinegar), cucumber, lentil, white bean or rice. They are all safely transportable from city to country in screw-top jars. Friday night's main course must travel easily and be in sufficient supply to possibly reappear at Saturday lunch in a somewhat different guise—frequent repeats are stuffed breast of veal, baked ham and barbecued loin of pork. A cold-weather specialty is chicken in white wine sauce. Serve it with linguine, which is cooked in rapidly boiling water at the final destination. A year-round cook-ahead favorite is a mountain of barbecued spareribs with coleslaw and beer. "That's the greatest kind of relaxing food—a real leveler—then everyone knows that there won't be a necktie worn all weekend." Here is one of Mrs. Spear's exemplary movable feasts:

Portable Cold Dinner or Lunch

Cold stuffed breast of veal (page 192) with garlic
   mayonnaise
Rice salad (page 182)
Cucumber salad
Italian whole-wheat bread with butter
Peaches

Out in East Hampton, Ruth relies heavily on her deep freeze and larder for homemade and store-bought delicacies. Each year she puts up vast quantities of produce from her own garden: pea soup, boxes of green pepper rings, apple and tomato sauces, jams, marmalades, etc. The freezer is stocked with fresh fruit pies and unfilled pie crusts, cookies, unusual breads and other bakery specialties from the city for Saturday and Sunday breakfasts.

"Our house policy for breakfast is unscheduled self-service. In the dining room there's a Salton hot tray plugged in with a pot of hot coffee, a pitcher of hot milk, and a basket of warmed croissants (kept on hand in the freezer)—they make people feel very cared for—or failing that, in an emergency, rusks which can be stored in an airtight tin. Also our own homemade marmalade, a pitcher of juice, and blueberries, when they're in season, with brown sugar and heavy cream."

Saturday lunch might either be a picnic at the beach, consumed from molded, indented plastic trays and plastic cups, or a lazy, easy meal such as cold roast chicken, coleslaw and melon balls with chopped crystallized ginger, or hard-boiled eggs, halved and masked in homemade mayonnaise, sliced tomatoes with basil, French bread and fresh fruit, all washed down with carafes of white wine. The children will be satisfied with hard-boiled-egg sandwiches, fruit and cookies. Because they love iced tea, Ruth doesn't bother carting a second thermos of milk down to the beach.

Even with a houseful of guests, Ruth is as likely to throw a spur-of-the-moment cocktail party in the country as in the city. Casual or not, however, she is "offended by farinaceous cocktail food," preferring crudités with curried mayonnaise dip, or French-fried zucchini sticks. Kielbasa picked up at the market may be poached in red wine and onions, sliced and served hot, or simply cooked in water and marinated in a vinaigrette sauce. Tiny new potatoes broken open and smothered in sour cream, a snippet of chives and a dab of caviar are a fast and certainly festive hors d'oeuvre.

Saturday night dinner is the first meal for which food need be bought while guests are in the house; "You want to shop once, load up the car, load up the fridge and *that's it.*" In the summer, fresh fish and vegetables are selected at local markets for a shore dinner of cold soup (prepared in the city and transported in a jar), baked striped bass perfumed with tarragon and stuffed with shrimp, mussels and mushrooms and white wine (page 190), and blueberry pie made with a home-frozen crust. This meal is neatly translated into Sunday lunch: cold bass with herbed mayonnaise, white bean salad (an "extender"), sliced tomatoes with purple onions and basil, fresh fruit and homemade cookies. However, if meat on a grill more suits the mood, Ruth might have brought out a marinated butterflied leg of lamb, which cooks as quickly as a thick steak. (It can also be run into a gas or electric grill with equally delicious results if the heavens decide to open.) Ruth has noticed that "grilling is part of the whole party. People like to help, and if everyone's allowed to get into the preparation of the food it makes a wonderfully relaxed atmosphere." Thus inspired, one might follow her lead with:

An Outdoor Dinner

Chilled pea and lettuce soup (page 180)
Barbecued marinated leg of lamb (page 195)
Sliced tomatoes with basil
Corn on the cob
Fresh raspberry pie (page 200)

Although Harvey and Ruth are both connoisseurs of rare wines, they think only unpretentious labels appropriate to casual country living. In the summer they buy Wente Brothers Blanc de Blanc and half-gallon cases of "all purpose" whites. Outdoors they are sipped from "those silvery plastic glasses—so pretty and cool—and which turn frosty when you fill them up with well-chilled wine. We always keep a mind-boggling reserve of bottles and jugs in an old fridge in the basement for . . . ah, well, you never know . . . for sudden summer *emergencies.*"

pauline trigère

For three decades, Pauline Trigère has stamped American fashion with her inimitable personal flair. To entertaining she brings the same aura of elegance and verve. Although one might easily mistake her for a one-woman fireworks display, Miss Trigère believes in poise and equilibrium: "I always look for beautiful balance. In clothes, in food, in my house, everywhere." This may well be the cornerstone of her extraordinary sense of style.

preferences

Dinners for 12 to 14 in the city, lunches for larger groups in the country.

atmosphere

Pauline is endowed with superhuman energy. "I love to cook. I think it's relaxing to come home after a late night and make the soup and dessert for a dinner party the next evening before going to bed. On weekends I sometimes spend four or five hours just doing the flowers."

In the city, a dinner guest is greeted with a booming welcome and ushered into a dazzling red on red enclosure—crimson felt walls, red and gold furniture, red pillows, red anemones, the hostess herself in a long drift of subtly spangled red chiffon. After drinks and hors d'oeuvres, including mushrooms marinated in a lavish vinaigrette with dry mustard, chopped herbs and hard-boiled eggs, the party moves across the hall into a pale drawing room clad in natural raw silks and bejeweled with pillows of dark obi fabrics, contemporary paintings, gold-framed drawings, ivories and Pauline's signature— her collection of turtles. In the Orient, she explains, the turtle symbolizes longevity, sturdiness and a trail of happiness. The turtle trademark appears on her paper cocktail-napkins, in her jewelry, on her tabletops—in every conceivable material and from every corner of the world. "It's amusing to have a collection with a single theme. It becomes part of you. As long as you don't become a slave to it—if you become a maniac about it it can get out of control. Once you've started, you can't just turn it off. After all these years

people are still bringing me turtles. I like to collect diamonds, but nobody believes me."

For the duration of the dinner, the drawing room is transformed into a glamorous dining room. Two tables, one a seven-foot-long semicircular mahogany drop-leaf console, the other a collapsible model skirted in an Indian print, are sumptuously set: "The looks of a table and the presentation of food are both terribly important. I'll use absolutely everything or anything for centerpieces." On Pauline's tables one may find galaxies of cut glass, dome-shaded candleholders, unmatched Limoges demitasse cups with a small bouquet in each, crystal elephants filled with flowers. For place cards, Pauline writes the guests' first names on brightly colored matchbooks.

In the country, a favorite decorative scheme is red geraniums. They are massed everywhere—on the terrace, on the lunch tables in low Oriental condiment dishes, and printed on the napkins. At Thanksgiving the table is covered with a huge display of vegetables and fruit—cabbages, eggplants, gourds, bananas, nuts, apples, grapes— "anything to suggest a harvest of plenty."

food and drink

On the subject of food, Pauline is decisive. "The trend is to simplicity. Too much elaboration is out. I hate chi-chi things en croûte and too many vegetables and sauces. In this apartment I have to be careful with cooking smells. I like to start with a soup. I have some beautiful green Japanese lacquer bowls with lids to keep the soup hot or cold. The butler sets it out and I call the guests to the table. For the main course everybody has to get up and go help themselves in the kitchen. In the meantime, the soup bowls are cleared away." In Pauline's stylish kitchen, patterned in green roses, the main course is set on a large marble-topped table. On the wall above it hangs a green blackboard emblazoned with the evening's menu in the hostess' distinctive rolling hand:

Dinner du 22 Avril

Soupe tortue ("turtle," but actually crab)
Le Navarin Pauline
La Salade Mélangée
Soufflé aux Oranges
Les Vins de France

The navarin is a meaty ragout of lean lamb, served surrounded by mounds of green peas, baby carrots, julienne green beans, tiny white turnips, small glazed onions and snow peas. The salad mates endive with beet. The frozen soufflé, sprinkled with grated zest and doused with Grand Marnier, is served with homemade cookies.

After dinner, the tables miraculously disappear, and coffee and liqueurs are served from a silver tray. Late to bed and early to rise is the motto in this household; drinks are once more offered after the demitasses are whisked away. The butler demands of the hostess, "Madame, may I bring you something to drink?" "Thank you, I'll have a glass of water with just a li-ttle float of Scotch." He returns with a highball. "Madame," he grins, "Scotch sinks."

nancy and derik power

Nancy Goslee Power is a distinguished young interior designer noted for her strikingly individual taste and her talent for infusing these hectic times with an aura of bygone grace and calm. Derik is an energetic English film producer whose career demands a considerable amount of business entertaining. Nancy was born in Delaware "Tidewater country" (as were "the Dutchess of Windsor, Pauline de Rothschild and Billy Baldwin—all marvelous party givers. Clearly we've got some kind of worthwhile tradition going for us"). Nancy, a superb hostess herself, has traveled widely, at one point living for two years in Tuscany. Today, to keep in touch with their families, friends and various professional interests, the Powers sprint with regularity from New York to Los Angeles, Delaware, Ireland, France, Italy and home again to their rosy Manhattan garden apartment (rosy at least for the moment, for as Nancy muses, "Now that it's finished, who knows what color it may be next month?").

preferences

Parties "of all kinds, shapes and sizes," with appropriate food and drink: Christmas open house, group effort "covered dish" suppers, spontaneous dinners, lazy late afternoon teas ("Teatime has no sexual connotation, and therefore it is much less threatening than a cocktail party"). "I love a festival . . . any occasion to have a real celebration. Birthdays, anniversaries, whatever." Nancy believes "the ambiance of a party must gratify all the senses, and it must change, like the menu, with the seasons."

The 1960's, Nancy feels, were the years of the "throwaway," when everything was disposable, and the future an existential void. "Now throwing things away is just not suitable. Our planet must be conserved. There is a new respect for quality and permanence. And calm. To me, calm today means turning the music off. Your ears can get more jaded than your palate. No Mick Jagger and eating your heart out and dancing before dinner—only after midnight."

Along with greater calm and respect for quality has come a greater sense of tradition: "I can't stand people who want to destroy traditions. We've been so used to a debased idea of Christmas that to suddenly have it flower again into a warm and moving occasion is a kind of miracle. The more knowledgeable and sophisticated a guest may be, the more I'll fall back on what I know from my own background. In Tidewater country," Nancy explains, "life was never as hard as it was in New England. The land was fertile, and the seas and rivers teemed with fish. Guests came to stay for weeks on end. The approach of a Tidewater host was very special—you always had to put your best foot forward. You held nothing back, kept nothing in reserve. Once you've been brought up that way, it's impossible to change. This doesn't mean gluttonous masses of food—it simply means giving the best you can find. I call my own cuisine 'Tidewater-Tuscan'—they both take the best from the countryside and keep it simple. The basic rule is to buy only the best and the freshest. And always in season."

On the need for seasonal change, Nancy is adamant. In summer she prefers furniture to be slipcovered in light fabrics, rugs rolled up and velvet pillows put away. She likes crisp cool cottons, pale colors, lemony scents, pots of herbs, straw and basketry, ferns, fresh fish and nasturtiums thrown in the salad. "Winter should smell of apple, pine, cinnamon, cloves and the heavier spices of the east." Every year she makes quantities of pomanders (page 159) and potpourri.

Nancy can't resist anything for the table: "I buy as many sets of china, silver and linen as I can sneak in the door." She advises the inexperienced host "always to keep on top of things—be sure to have more glasses than you need, and buy things for the table when you see them. Don't wait—you'll never be able to find them on the day of the party, you can be sure." In summer she decorates her tables with pots of herbs, or baskets of Chinese vegetables. She might use brown eggs at Easter, and ribbons, candles and pots of potpourri at every place for Christmas dinner. She feels that the greatest inspiration always comes spontaneously. "Look in your closet. Don't be intimidated by lack of equipment. More than once, a new garbage can has served as an ice-bucket. Of course, you should try to be well equipped, but don't worry if you're not. Just *do it.*"

Nancy also prefers a spontaneous guest list. She has noticed that the more she labors over one, the more likely a party will fail to take off. Inviting guests who share a single milieu or interest (writers, movie people or whatever) also may result in social frost or downright mayhem. And Nancy never tells her guests that dress will be casual or informal. Like other hostesses she finds that this term may mean blue jeans to one and something long but simple to another, to everyone's mutual embarrassment. She feels that one should always dress for dinner, "even if it only means putting on a special pair of earrings. But no jeans!"

food and drink

When planning a menu, Nancy is keenly aware of contrasting colors and textures. "Although I plan ahead, I keep it totally flexible so I can work in whatever looks freshest at the market. You see, I'm always thinking in terms of seasons. One of these New Year's Eves, I'd like to go diamonds and black velvet all the way, with tons of oysters on the half shell and a lot of divinely seasonal fresh caviar. Oh, well, dreaming about it is almost as much fun." In the meantime, here are a few of Nancy's tempting menus:

For a summer dinner, served with a dry white wine:

Broiled bluefish with lemon butter
Tomatoes stuffed with rice
Green salad with nasturtium flowers
Strawberry tart

For a last-minute autumn celebration with champagne:

Smoked salmon
Spinach and Parmesan soufflé
Field salad with lemon and oil
Oranges in spiced red wine

For Christmas, when Nancy's been known to assemble eighteen guests ("friends, house guests, extras, strays, homeless fathers, you name it—everyone felt like a family and acted like one") for a great seated holiday dinner embracing both the Powers' culinary traditions, Tidewater and English, the feast included:

157

Cream of sorrel soup
Country ham
Roast goose stuffed with prunes, apricots, apples
   and green grapes
Brussel sprouts with butter sauce
Wild rice
Plum pudding with brandy sauce and the tradi-
   tional English sixpence buried within

Nancy has rediscovered another traditional form of entertaining. She recently solved the problem of dinner before a charity dance by initiating an updated "covered dish supper," an ideal solution for a widely assorted group, many of whom did not know each other. "It's an excellent kind of party to ease the timid out of their shells, and for the young who feel socially apprehensive in the company of glib and unfamiliar older people. The host need merely set the scene and let it happen. But there must be no display or sense of competition. Each guest or couple should be told what category of food to bring, or what specific course, but the host should not be dictatorial or overly organized. But you've got to give them poetic license to use their imaginations. There needn't be too many hot dishes, even in the winter, so there should be little competition for oven space. "Cold" foods should not be overchilled. Many dishes, such as bean or rice salads, sliced meats, grilled fowl and piperades are good at tepid "room" temperature.

On one particular occasion, there were no oven-heated dishes at all. The hostess contributed a salade Niçoise vinaigrette, a salade Danoise of cooked peas and mushrooms in curried mayonnaise, and a ratatouille. A photographer brought a seafood risotto, a non-cooking young designer a Bloomingdale's pâté, an art dealer brought prosciutto and melon. Dessert consisted of strawberries with oceans of cream, again supplied by the hostess.

Guests may occasionally be allowed to help prepare a meal, but there the community effort ends: "When the time comes to clear away, my motto is stack, but don't shovel. I absolutely refuse to let anyone help me clean up. The only time I've had things broken is when I've had other people insist on helping clean up. The last time, and the very last, four of my best plates went in one fell swoop.

In conclusion, Nancy points to two happy side benefits rarely brought up in discussions on entertaining. The first: "When all the guests have gone, I always study the way the living room chairs are left. This suggests what may be the best seating arrangements for the future." The second: "I clean up for myself as well as my friends. If I didn't give a lot of parties, the apartment might never be clean. Yes, if I have to, I'll stuff things under the bed, but I don't care if anybody sees. The one thing I've learned to eliminate when giving a party is fear—I tossed fear out the door."

Nancy Goslee Power's
Recipe for Pomander Balls

Oranges, lemons or apples
3 tablespoons powdered cinnamon
1 tablespoon powdered nutmeg
1 tablespoon orrisroot
1 tablespoon powdered cardamom
Whole cloves—approximately 2 oz. per fruit

"Mix the powdered spices together in a shallow dish. Stick the whole cloves into the fruit, rather close together; the fruit does shrink when dry, so leaving a tiny space between cloves is all right. Roll the fruit in the spices. Wrap the ball in tissue paper and put it in a cool, dry place for several weeks to season. When you're ready to use it, tie it up with plaid ribbons—or anything pretty—to hang in closets, pile in an old basket, or put in an English pottery jar, made especially for pomanders. Makes the house smell wonderful for parties."

marjorie and harold reed

Art dealer Harold Reed and his wife Margie, as she is known by all her friends, live with their small son Bradford in a sprawling New York town house, which also serves as Mr. Reed's gallery. They enjoy entertaining and plan parties together down to the last intricate detail. Marjorie devotes as much effort to table settings and decorations as she does to her inventive and varied menus: "My greatest passion in the whole world is arranging flowers before a party."

preferences

Lunches, dinners, garden parties, receptions, kitchen parties, preferably for 20 or more: "With twenty there needn't be any worry about people getting along. Everyone will find somebody they enjoy. The more mixed a bag you can get, the better. People like to change company and move around. They like to sit in different places and look at different things."

atmosphere

Chagalls, Boteros, Dubuffets, Bacons, Lindners sing out against a background of peach, mauves, pinks and greens. The Reeds see their house as not only a setting for paintings and sculpture but for people: "If guests have gone to the trouble to get themselves together, we want them to be seen to their best advantage. That's why we start an evening with bright lights—so that people aren't stumbling around in the dark or getting lost in the shadows." At dinner the guests are flattered by the light of literally dozens of candles, either in hurricane lamps on the tables, or scattered about in low, votive cups. The romantic mood is carried back upstairs after dinner, in a candlelit drawing room. Visual moods are plotted with the same care that a stage designer would lavish on a set. Whether the final effect is dramatic, romantic or even witty, guests will be made to feel an electrically festive excitement. Margie has designed the interiors with an eye to sudden surprise as people move from one kind of ambiance into another—there is an

161

Italianate roof garden with a built-in brick grill and groaning flower boxes, a wrought-iron balustraded terrace with French windows leading into the house and a view of the leafy garden, a "night-club room" for dancing, a library with a grand piano, a drawing room paneled in mauve-tinted boiseries, a huge subterranean Spanish-tiled kitchen fitted out with antique armoires and a cooking island, where at buffets guests may help themselves (not one, but two other kitchens can be found on upper floors of the house).

The Reed dining room is large enough to accommodate several round tables. When decorating, Margie takes inspiration from the season, the market, or from the uncharted regions of her imagination: "The rules are finished, completely *finished* on what has to be on informal or formal tables. For example, I want all my glasses to be chic but inexpensive, like those wonderful oversized stemmed wine goblets that you can even use for desserts. We want everyone to relax, so we put out big square ashtrays and china and glass that is never so valuable it can't be broken. It's all part of getting away from the formal, precious look. We've found terrific bamboo flatware, and Lucite, which looks great in the kitchen or on the terrace."

"We're also sick and tired of million-dollar Porthault table linen. Now we think in terms of mood. For formal dinners we still love white eyelet cloths over beautiful solid colors. On the roof, though, I might decide to cover the tables with natural burlap cloths and make centerpieces of candles, sand, sea shells and driftwood with flowers arranged to look as if they're growing out of the crevices. Or I use an American Indian theme with Navajo bowls, cactus and succulents. Or ivy and miniature roses for a garden party. Or I could go crazy with orchids—orchids are my favorite flower. Flowering plants are great because they last so much longer than cut flowers.

Margie, who creates her arrangements the day before a party, has an extraordinary way with plants and flowers. (She confides that a few tablespoons of sugar in the vase will persuade peonies or tulips to open, and that she feeds Sprite to roses.) She collects tiny glass vials and Chinese vases to hold a single bud at each place setting or small bunches of flowers to create the effect of a fantastic formal garden running down the length of the dining room table. Or she may girdle terra-cotta pots of hyacinths with knotted gingham napkins. "Whatever we decide on, though, it will be loose and natural, not tight and pushed together." Hal agrees: "Don't you hate that stiff catered flower look? You go to someone's house, and they've sent out for everything—everything's there, but without *really* being there, if you know what I mean. There's been no *thought* behind it, no *caring.* It's kind of an insult. You ask yourself, what did these people do except spend a lot of money? And why? Just to get rid of a lot of pay-backs?"

At the Reeds', wine bottles are always wrapped in a napkin: "Nothing comes to the table undressed." Margie has no interest in silver salvers and conventional serving pieces. She loves the texture and feathery weight of baskets, and lines them with bright napkins whenever possible. Bread is served in baskets, and a three-tiered basket bears a burden of fresh fruit. At cocktail parties, thin tea sandwiches, "which don't wreck your house," are handed around in flat baskets decorated with gardenias ("Hal loves leaves and flowers together with food"), and *coeur à la crème* is also served in a basket, a gingham napkin cushioning the dish. Cheeses are served on flat platter-like baskets lined with leaves. And they like unusual food presentation: cold soup or chicken salad may appear in abalone shells, peaches and honey in giant champagne goblets, cold lemon soufflés in small, individual clay flower pots. "So many people are on diets, we usually have a fruit of some sort at lunch—but with delicate cookies fresh from the oven for anyone who likes. On second thought, most people do." The Reeds' recipe for chocolate meringue cookies provides ample explanation (page 200).

remi saunder

Remi Saunder, a warm and witty Russian émigré, shares a New York apartment, at once compact and airily romantic, with an affectionate snowpile of Siberian Samoyeds, both resident and guest. Over the last few years, her quarters have evolved into a kind of elegant commune where Mrs. Saunder runs seemingly nonstop open house for streams of friends, Slavic and otherwise, punctuated on weekends by hale and hearty Russian "high teas."

preferences

High teas, and occasional "before or after the performance" suppers.

Remi loves the free-form simplicity of high teas. For more organized gatherings, she looks for a launching pad of some sort: "I get more stimulated at my own parties if they have a theme, a raison d'être. Automatically it makes a festive atmosphere, whether it's New Year's Eve or Valentine's Day, a birthday, a visit from a friend from abroad, a book that's just been published or someone's concert. Sundays, though, are simply to be with your friends—*they're* the theme. That's why tea is so nice."

atmosphere

Remi's surroundings, both animate and inanimate, intriguingly chart her life, with its abrupt transitions from Russia to Europe to England and then on once again to America. Stepping through a foyer like a malachite cave, one enters the living room, its walls also gleaming greenly beneath a stippled glaze. "I've painted the whole place food colors—look at these walls, a wonderful spinach soufflé—and those in there, what do you think? Peach? Salmon? Maybe melon? Who knows. Anyway, *I* think it looks absolutely delicious. And here's the kitchen—just look—chocolate mousse and whipped cream! I hope it makes everybody good and hungry!"

164

In the living room, cascades of paintings, designs from the Russian ballet, porcelain animals, candle-filled sconces, carved ivories, dim baroque mirrors spill down the walls and over marble-topped, lacquer and silk-skirted tables. Also on prominent display are Remi's shiny white bicycle, handlebars gaily festooned with fake flowers, two splendid Mother Russian samovars and a flotilla of photographic portraits inscribed by their famous subjects. The faces and flying feet are impressive—"Slava" Rostropovich, his daughters and wife, Galina Vishnevskaya, "Misha" Baryshnikov, "Rudi" Nureyev, to mention only a few of Remi's "regulars." More often than not at least one of them will be found somewhere in the depths of a couch or chair talking vociferously while downing endless glass cups of tea from the gurgling samovar. (Today samovars can be electrified, although traditionally they are heated by a central unit filled with smoldering charcoal. To dilute the super-strong tea essence, which is kept warm in a little pot enthroned on top of the mechanism, hot water is drawn off through a spigot beneath the samovar's belly. An acceptable substitute can be a pot of tea essence atop a trivet-candle warmer and a carafe or pot of scalding hot water.)

An innate talent for flexibility has helped vanquish problems of housing equipment and supplies in limited space. Taking advantage of her high ceilings, Remi hired a carpenter to build a wine rack over a hallway door; over a second one he installed simple cabinets large enough to store card tables and folding chairs. A collapsible round tabletop for seated dinners for eight slips easily into a closet. In the kitchen, clearly labeled, brightly colored boxes are stacked efficiently on top of tall cabinets. A long marble-topped sideboard, with excellent storage space below, stands sensibly opposite the kitchen door. Lightweight gilt French side chairs make child's play of spontaneous groupings. Remi refuses to let herself become compulsively tidy: "When it's time for a party and everything's not in order, I shove all problems under the rug. I'm the rug."

While teas are her trademark, Remi tries periodically to alter the formula. "If you do give a lot of teas, you have to vary the menu somewhat for friends who come frequently." Tea itself poses certain problems; it can either kill the taste of some foods (it makes most seafood taste unpleasantly fishy, for example) or, in turn, it can be swamped by overly powerful flavors. A high tea as served by Mrs. Saunder will always include a salt and a sweet course. Fresh plates will be brought out only if the first course has been "too messy or cheesy." Typically a menu will follow these guidelines, including a sampling of the following categories:

Some meat: pâté, chopped liver, rolled ham slices with parsley sprigs, smoked sausage, salami, cold sliced leftover meat loaf, chicken or duck.

Some cheese: Feta or other mild goat cheese, Gruyère, a ripe King Christian, Bel Paese, Edam.

Some breads: Black or whole-grain pumpernickel, French bread, croissants, toasted Italian pannetone or "Sahara" bread, seedless rye, English or corn muffins (the last from a mix), Norwegian flatbread, scones, popovers.

Sweet butter and jam: sour cherry only (which is to Russians what madeleines were to Proust).

Piroshki: Small Russian pastry turnovers either stuffed with meat (page 193) or cabbage fillings or with jam or sweetened cooked apples. Served warm.

Sweets: Fruit tarts, cakes, Napoleons, coffee cakes.

Tea: Russian, but sometimes 2 parts Earl Grey to 3 parts Darjeeling, brewed very strong.

Other stand-bys: Hard-boiled eggs, peeled but otherwise unadorned, shavings of fresh horseradish, chopped dill.

In spring, Remi might precede the tea with individual bowls of cucumber, radish, sour cream and dill salad. In winter, there will always be hot piroshki, which have the added attraction of freezing well. At Easter time, all these are supplanted by two monumental holiday specialties—*kulich,* a stout sugar-glazed column of fruit-bejeweled brioche, and *paskha* (page 197), a towering molded confection made of sweetened farmer's cheese, vanilla, currants and minced almonds.

There is a cue we might all take from Remi's general food philosophy. "It's usually really a question of how much money you want to spend and how many people you've asked. Bread can be just as tasty as croissants, and this does help your pocketbook. So if you can't afford pâté, buy some good liverwurst." On the subject of waste she is firm. "I've seen enough hardship in the world, so I can't tolerate it. I keep cheeses carefully wrapped in Saran in the refrigerator, also pumpernickel, which is my favorite bread—it can keep for weeks. With all breads I only cut a minimum amount so that it stays as fresh as possible on its board. I always try to avoid sandwiches—they're a lot of work at the last minute, it's difficult to calculate how many you'll need, but worst of all they're usually wasteful. I want people to think that they can take as much as they want, but without wasting it. That's why I like to use bunches of parsley to decorate a dinner table, or all apples, or all lemons, especially if you have a lemony soup or dessert—afterwards you can eat them all up."

Remi's sympathetic devotion to animals extends to food and decorations: "I'd never serve real foie gras—force feeding of geese is strictly against my principles. And now I'm so freaked out about all this business about sensitive plants that even cut flowers are beginning to make me feel, well—nervous. But I like plants on the dinner table, again you don't waste. I think with party decorations you have to make sense out of nonsense—little Chinese paper favors are inexpensive and fun. It depends on your mood. For a rustic dinner like pork chops, for place cards I've written guests' names on wooden cooking spoons to take home with them as souvenirs. But basically if you have good food, you don't have to worry about other things. An old Russian friend here in New York says it doesn't matter where you live—just nail a steak to the front door and everyone will come."

gael greene

Gael Greene, *New York* magazine's Insatiable Critic, metamorphoses into the Incorrigible Romantic when broached on the subject of entertaining.

preferences

Like all true Romantics, Gael tends to think in terms of the ideal. Her ideal party? "The one where you meet a man who becomes part of your life for some glorious period of time." Then, let's put it another way. What has Ms. Greene found to be the ideal form of party and number of guests when she entertains at home? "Dinner for two. All right, if it *must* be expanded, eight seems a good number."

atmosphere

No matter what the number, the mood must be relaxed: "The most terrible party is the one where the hostess or host—or worse, both—are over their heads. I know. I've given a few myself. The tension becomes sicker than a bad rice pudding. You must be comfortable to cope. That's why it's so much easier for a couple to give a party than someone single—they support each other in the face of disaster and can accomplish what one person on the verge of hysteria can't pull off single-handedly."

For the single-handed host, what does she suggest to foster calm? "After fighting it for years, I've come to the conclusion that it's a very good idea to invest money in help, even if you have to cut down on flowers or expensive wine. Whatever the sacrifice, it also means doing without a lot of nerve-racking toil and trouble. Get somebody good to serve and clean up, and you can concentrate on your guests instead of kitchen logistics. You also escape the Cinderella syndrome—once a party's over, there's no more glorious feeling than to find all those dishes magically clean and ready to put away. Particularly if someone, well, interesting has stayed on after the others have left."

Gael finds she feels less like Cinderella in her country home, where kitchen, dining and living room are all in one: "You become the center of the party." But she is aware of its potential hazards. A kitchen has a perverse tendency to become a mess. "It is also like being on stage." Silent onlookers can occasionally fluster even the most unflappable of chefs. Should this happen, culinary battle plans may start to go awry, a situation which she claims may be turned to advantage: "One of the best dinners I can remember is where the pheasant took longer than expected. Although I generally think that one or maybe two drinks should be the limit before dinner, this disaster gave people time for an extra. They were so happy by the time we got to actually confront the birds, it turned into a beautiful evening."

A convivial atmosphere, she hastens to add, should ideally be sparked by personal rather than alcoholic chemistry. "The people, after all, are the whole point. That's why to me the ideal guest is the one who can talk to anybody." How does she compose a guest list? "No snobs. No stiffs. Ideally I'd include some great storytellers, some beautiful women, some beautiful men, some naughty married friends as well as some freshly single ones to heighten the potential for intrigue. At least a couple of them would have to be good listeners. There's nothing worse than a roomful of stars and no one to appreciate them.

"Even if they're all extroverts, though, they'll probably need a little help to hit it off. I hate to be greeted by a host and abandoned. Particularly at the beginning of a party, people whom the host thinks will get on should be brought together. It helps to be told at least something about a person whom you're meeting for the first time. A full job resumé isn't necessary. Just a few clues to get the conversation going. Some indication of a person's interests or tastes will do. Even marital status, if you like to be a matchmaker. Point out all the lovely possibilities. How? By getting to the point and saying, Here you are, that one's good, yes and that one. It's unforgivable to leave a woman trapped in the clutches of some lecherous married man who's going to break her heart in six months. Especially if there was an alternative."

But simply assembling the right mix of guests and introducing them informatively isn't enough. "At dinner you have to seat people with a chemist's eye to maximum intrigue and interest. I always separate lovers as well as mates. Married couples should be kept

170

as far away from each other as possible. Being forced out of stultifying domestic forms can give each of them an exciting lift. It's a terrific break for a husband whose wife interrupts all his sentences. Also he can tell a joke she's heard nineteen times without her groaning. Meanwhile she can be outrageously flirtatious. Who knows? Maybe she'll come home feeling sexier than she has in weeks."

As a professional food critic, what are Ms. Greene's thoughts on menus for entertaining? "A menu you can handle comfortably. Seasonal foods. Avoid dinner-party clichés. Personally, I like to serve sinful food to my friends. I'm probably guilty of threatening countless lives of men over forty with the content of what I cook. Fettucine dripping with cream. And butter. And cheese. If I've also made an infamously lethal chocolate dessert, I do try to offer fresh fruit as well. Then they can decide for themselves what's good for them. But if I had to lay down one guiding law, I'd definitely say that it's better to have mediocre food and fascinating, outgoing guests than a gastronomic tour de force and a bunch of monosyllabic stiffs!"

recipes

Helen McCully's Chicken Liver Pâté

½ pound chicken livers	A few sprigs of parsley, minced
2 tablespoons butter	¾ teaspoon salt
2 hard-cooked eggs, shelled	2 or 3 twists of the pepper mill
1 package (8-ounce size) cream cheese, softened	2 tablespoons of cognac

Heat the butter in a heavy skillet. When hot, add the chicken livers and sauté until they are lightly brown outside but still somewhat pink inside. To determine this, cut one open. Chop fairly fine. Work the livers and the hard-cooked eggs through a meat grinder, using the finest blade; or purée in the electric blender or food processor. Grind or purée a second time to make a very smooth mixture.

Work the cheese until very soft and malleable. Best done with your hands. Then work in the liver mixture, parsley, salt, and cognac thoroughly. Makes about 1½ cups.

Spoon it into a suitable serving dish, and seal with Saran or dress it up with a coating of aspic. A seal is important because the pâté darkens when exposed to air. Serve with dry or buttered toast points or unseasoned crackers.

To make the aspic: Sprinkle 1 envelope of unflavored gelatin over ½ cup cold water to soften. Combine this with 1 can of consommé (10½-ounce size) in a saucepan and stir over a low heat until dissolved. Pour a ¼-inch layer of the aspic on top of the pâté and refrigerate until firm—a couple of hours possibly. This is attractive if the pâté is to be served for a "cocktail."

This pâté cannot be frozen because of the eggs.

Since most of the aspic will be left over, refrigerate it and use it up some other way. For instance, melt over low heat, refrigerate until the mixture has the consistency of unbeaten egg whites, then combine with cooked vegetables diced small. Pour into a mold and refrigerate until firm. Good with mayonnaise and sliced cold meat.

James Beard's Pâté
de Campagne, Provençale

2 pounds lean pork, very coarsely chopped
2 pounds veal, chopped rather finely
1 pound ground pork liver
1 pound fresh pork siding or fat bacon, diced
6 garlic cloves, minced
3 eggs

½ teaspoon Spice Parisienne
⅓ cup cognac or whiskey
1 tablespoon basil
1 tablespoon salt (approximately)
1 teaspoon freshly ground black pepper
Bacon or salt pork (enough to line the terrine)

Combine all the meats and seasonings. If you wish to test the seasoning, sauté a small piece—about 1 tablespoon—in butter till it's cooked through.

Line a good-sized straight-sided terrine or baking dish with salt pork or bacon. A 2½-quart soufflé dish, heavy pottery dish or a large round Pyrex dish is ideal. Fill it with the mixture and form a well-rounded top. Place a few strips of bacon or salt pork over the top, and bake at 325° for 2 to 2½ hours. I always cover it with a sheet of foil for the first hour or so of cooking. It will break away from the sides a bit when done.

Remove it from the oven and cool. Weight it down after the first half-hour of cooling. Serve from the terrine or dish in generous slices with a sharp, heavy knife. Cover tightly with foil when replaced in the refrigerator.

The Novecks' Eggplant Beignets

1 medium (about 1 pound) eggplant
¼ cup water
1 egg beaten, plus 1 beaten white
½ teaspoon salt
½ teaspoon pepper

1 small grated onion
⅓ cup flour
1 teaspoon baking powder
Oil for frying (about 1 inch)

Peel and cube the eggplant. Covered, cook it in water till tender. Mash, stir in the egg, onion, salt, pepper and baking powder. Add the beaten egg white. Heat the oil in a large frying pan. Drop the batter in by spoonfuls and cook till brown. Drain and sprinkle with parsley.

Can be kept warm in 200° oven. Can also be made with zucchini, potatoes, etc.

The Batterberrys' Marinated Shrimp

Into sufficient water to cover 1 to 2 pounds of shrimp (approximately 30 to 60 cocktail size) drop 2 thin slices of lemon, 3 tablespoons of wine vinegar, a dozen peppercorns, a bay leaf, a large pinch of thyme, and a dash of Tabasco. Bring to a boil, simmer 5 minutes and plunge in the shrimp. Bring to the boiling point once again and immediately turn off the heat. Let the shrimp cool for at least 20 to 30 minutes in their broth. Meanwhile, prepare the marinade:

½ cup oil (¼ cup olive oil, ¼ cup salad oil)
½ cup dry white wine
Juice of 2 lemons (about a generous ½ cup)
1 teaspoon sugar
1 tablespoon kosher salt
3 tablespoons freshly grated horseradish (or 2½ of bottled)

1 cup finely minced celery hearts, including leaves
⅔ cup finely minced scallions
⅔ cup minced Italian parsley
A dozen twists of the black pepper mill

Combine all the ingredients in order given, stirring with each addition. When the shrimp are cool enough to handle (yet still warm) shell and de-vein, but leave the tail intact. Marinate for 2 to 4 hours in the refrigerator. If the marinade seems too soupy for serving with toothpicks, strain off some of the excess juices before arranging in a bowl. If compelled to use flash-frozen shrimp, follow directions, drain immediately, pat dry, and submerge in the marinade while still hot.

Bruce Sinclair's Croque Monsieur

16 slices of bread (crusts off)
16 slices of Gruyère cheese
8 slices of Virginia ham
2 eggs

½ cup dry sherry
Water
Butter

Make sandwiches of bread, cheese, ham, cheese and bread, and fasten with toothpicks. Beat eggs well, add sherry, beat again, add just enough water—no more than ¼ cup—until the batter reaches the right consistency for French toast. Dip the sandwiches in the egg mixture, sauté in melted butter over low heat in an electric skillet (or, having none, a regular frying pan), turning frequently until golden brown—the cheese should be softly melted. Cut into quarters, remove the toothpicks, sprinkle with crumbled bacon and surround with crisp sprigs of watercress.

The Batterberrys'
Camembert Mousse

To make 1 pound:

2 4-ounce half-moons or 1 8-ounce wheel of
    Camembert
2 sticks (½ pound) sweet butter

6 tablespoons dry vermouth
3 or 4 good squirts of Tabasco
Toasted almonds, finely or coarsely chopped

Trim the crust from the cheese with a small, very sharp knife. This operation can be made easier by running the cheese into the freezer for 10 to 15 minutes to stiffen the white rind. Cut the cheese into small cubes. Let the butter soften to room temperature and beat until light and fluffy. Mash the softened cheese to a paste in a separate bowl and gradually beat in the butter. When melded, slowly beat in the vermouth and Tabasco—we say *slowly*, otherwise the solids and liquids will not amalgamate. The consistency should be that of overly thick mayonnaise. With a rubber spatula, shape more or less into the form of a wheel of cheese in the center of a large round plate. Refrigerate. When firm, cover the mousse heavily with the chopped almonds, pressing them in with the fingertips. Tidy up the plate. Serve as a spread surrounded with dry toast squares or Carr's water biscuits. Note: If you own a food processor, you might very well consider going into the Camembert Mousse business.

Toasted Salted Almonds

Dribble a fine film of cooking oil over the bottom of a heavy skillet, then, over medium heat, pan-toast whole blanched almonds, shaking the pan vigorously from time to time to avoid scorching. When they turn a rich beige shade, drain the nuts on paper towels, sprinkle with kosher salt and serve while still warm. As this last step will probably not be convenient, run them into a hot oven for a minute or so to reheat just before serving.

The Batterberrys' Bagna Cauda

(A warm dip for raw vegetable sticks, strips and flowerets.)

5 to 6 anchovy fillets

3 to 4 cloves of garlic

6 tablespoons sweet butter

6 tablespoons olive oil

1 cup chopped white truffles (or truffle substitute—see below)

Soak the anchovies for 5 minutes in warm, but not hot, water. Rinse, drain, dry and mash with a fork. Crush the garlic into mixture of melted butter and oil. Over very low heat, stir and let steep for 5 to 6 minutes; *do not let the garlic brown*. Add anchovies.

Stir in the truffles or this substitute:

6 tablespoons dried mushrooms

1 pound fresh mushrooms

¼ cup olive oil

1½ shallots

½ clove garlic

¼ teaspoon black pepper

¼ teaspoon white pepper

Salt

Soak the dried mushrooms for ½ to 1 hour in scalding water. Discard the fresh mushroom stems and slice the caps. Over high heat, sauté the sliced mushrooms in hot olive oil for approximately 15 minutes, or until they lightly brown and expel their moisture. After the first 10 minutes of sautéeing, add the drained, dried and finely chopped dry mushrooms. Crush the shallots and garlic with a pestle or in a garlic press and drop into a small bowl. Scrape the mushrooms from the pan into the bowl, mix well, season with pepper and salt to taste, and let stand at room temperature for at least 12 hours. Makes about 1 cup.

To assemble the bagna cauda, put anchovy-garlic-butter-oil-truffle or truffle substitute into a small chafing dish. Keep hot. Arrange pieces of raw vegetables around it or nearby for dunking.

The Novecks' Dilled Crêpes and Fillings

¾ cup each of flour and milk

3 eggs

¼ cup water

½ teaspoon salt

2 tablespoons cooled melted butter

3 tablespoons snipped dill

The crêpes: Blend ingredients up to and including the ½ teaspoon salt in blender for 30 seconds at high speed. Scrape down. Add 2 tablespoons cooled melted butter, blend a few seconds more. Transfer the batter to a bowl. Stir in 3 tablespoons dill. Cover, let stand at least 1 hour.

Heat a seasoned 6-inch crêpe pan. Brush lightly with clarified butter, and with a measuring cup, pour in batter until pan is half full, plus a little. Pour into pan, swirling to cover bottom. Return excess, if any, to batter bowl. Cook about 30 to 40 seconds over moderate heat; turn, cook less time to complete cooking. Transfer to plate.

To store crêpes, for hours, or even months, in the freezer, put wax paper between each crêpe, cover with foil, and freeze. To heat after freezing, puncture holes in the foil, to allow any steam to escape, and heat in a slow oven. Yield: about 20 crêpes.

The Novecks' Crêpe Fillings

Fillings: Smoked salmon, cream cheese: 8 oz. cream cheese, ½ lb. salmon, 3 tablespoons béchamel sauce. Spread a layer of cheese, and cover with salmon. Fold, and seam side down, lay in buttered ovenproof dish. Dot with butter, and heat slowly, to avoid drying out of the salmon. Spread with béchamel sauce, and parsley sprigs. Serve.

Also a very rich and good filling: 1 to 1¼ cups ricotta, 2 to 4 tablespoons fresh grated Parmesan, ½ cup finely cubed mortadella, ½ cup finely cubed prosciutto, salt and pepper. Mix ingredients. Fill crêpes, cover with 4 to 6 tablespoons melted butter, and cover with foil. Bake at 325° about 25 minutes until heated. Top with grated Parmesan, and serve.

Ruth Spear's Chilled
Pea and Lettuce Soup

One 10-ounce box of frozen peas, partially
 thawed, or 1¼ cups shelled fresh peas
1 medium potato, diced
1 medium onion, chopped
1 head of Boston lettuce, quartered

2 cups chicken broth or stock
1 cup heavy cream
Juice of ½ lemon
Salt, freshly ground pepper
Mint, optional

Put peas, potato, onion, lettuce, and 1 cup of the chicken broth in a saucepan. Bring to the boil. Lower heat, cover, and simmer 10 minutes.

Pour into a blender jar and blend until vegetables are puréed. Return to the saucepan, add the remaining cup of stock, and simmer 5 minutes. Add cream and lemon juice, and season to taste with salt and pepper. Chill. Garnish with mint.

Luisa-Esther Flynn's
Gazpacho Andaluz—for 6

2 pounds very ripe tomatoes
1 sweet red pepper
½ cucumber, seeded
1 clove garlic, optional

3 slices crustless bread moistened generously
    with olive oil
1 tablespoon red vinegar
Salt and pepper

Take first five ingredients and purée in batches in the blender. Strain through a sieve. Chill for 4 to 5 hours in the refrigerator. An hour before serving add 4 or 5 ice cubes. Serve soup in chilled cups and pass separate bowls of these garnishes: chopped, seeded cucumber, minced green pepper, and small croutons.

Salade Niçoise

While there are many variations played on this specialty of the French Riviera, the basic ingredients should always include: flaked, oil-packed tuna; rinsed anchovy fillets; peeled tomato wedges or cherry tomatoes; sauce vinaigrette. Optional: lettuce, cooked green beans, cold sliced potatoes, capers, thin purple onion rings or scallions, cucumber, chopped herbs. If potatoes are used, lettuce is usually omitted. A specialty of Bloomingdale's "Forty Carrots" restaurants is a sesame-scented variation on the salade niçoise theme: tender young spinach leaves, chunks of tuna, walnuts and cherry tomatoes are tossed in a dressing made of equal parts of dark sesame oil, corn oil and red wine vinegar seasoned with salt and pepper, a whiff of minced garlic and a pinch each of sugar, paprika, celery seed, dried fines herbes and basil.

Ruth Spear's Rice Salad

3 cups hot cooked white rice (not instant)
½ cup olive oil (can be a mixture of the oil in the artichoke jar and regular olive oil)
½ pound fresh mushrooms
3 tablespoons butter
1 cup sliced marinated artichoke hearts (available in jars)

1 cup fresh tomatoes, peeled, seeded and chopped
½ cup sliced black olives
1 teaspoon freshly cracked black pepper
Salt
½ purple onion, thinly sliced

Toss the hot rice with the oil in a large bowl, using 2 forks. Set aside to cool.

Slice the mushrooms thin and sauté briefly in the butter. Add them to the rice along with the artichoke hearts, tomatoes, olives, pepper, salt to taste, and onion, and toss well again. Serve at room temperature. Makes 6 portions.

Variation: If fresh tomatoes are not available, slivers of sweet red peppers, either fresh or canned, make an agreeable substitute.

The Batterberrys' Salade Composée with Baked Beets

1½ to 2 cups of sliced baked beets
4 large branches of celery cut in julienne
¾ pound Gruyère or aged Swiss cheese cut in fine julienne
1 bunch watercress
3 large or 4 small Belgian endives and 2 or 3 handfuls of chicory
¾ cup olive oil plus two tablespoons

1 lemon
1 tablespoon wine vinegar
1 heaping tablespoon Dijon mustard, extra strong
White pepper
Tabasco
Kosher salt
4 cloves garlic

Bake the beets, loosely wrapped in foil, in a 375–400° oven until their centers are easily pierced with a skewer. According to the size of the beets, this may take as long as 3½ to 4 hours. When they are cool, peel them and slice thin into bite-sized pieces. Moisten with 2 tablespoons of olive oil and sprinkle with salt. Peel and halve the garlic cloves, pierce with toothpicks and stir them around in the beets. Cover with plastic and marinate for several hours, jiggling the bowl occasionally. Discard the garlic before serving.

Trim the celery of coarse strings and cut into matchsticks. Refrigerate.

Marinate the julienne of cheese in mustard dressing: the heaping tablespoon of extra strong Dijon, ½ cup olive oil, 1 tablespoon wine vinegar, juice of ½ lemon, a dozen grinds of white pepper, 6 drops of Tabasco. Refrigerate.

Trim the endive, split lengthwise and slice crosswise into bite-sized pieces. Toss in ⅛ cup olive oil, juice of ¼ lemon, and season lightly with salt and pepper just before composing the salad.

Trim the watercress and break the chicory into small pieces. Arrange the greens, endive, cheese, celery and beets attractively in a large bowl and toss thoroughly at the table.

Naomi Graffman's Guarneri Salad

This is for 8 to 12 portions or more, depending upon size of same.

2 cups cooked, cut-up shrimp
2 cups cooked, cubed chicken
2 cups cooked, cubed spicy salami or kielbasa or ham*

2 cups raw zucchini (skin left on), cubed
½ cup capers
1 cup finely chopped pimento
2 cups cooked barley

Toss all this together with green sauce, made as follows:

Bunch of parsley
Bunch of fresh basil (a handful, about equal to parsley) or a goodly quantity of dried basil
Anchovies (3 or 4, to taste)

⅓ cup fresh lemon juice
⅓ cup tarragon vinegar
2 cups salad oil
Freshly ground pepper

Put lemon juice and vinegar into blender; blend with greens and anchovies and then add oil gradually. Season to taste.

After the salad is tossed and seasoned, refrigerate overnight. (Note: in order that it marinate properly, it's best to store it in a long and flattish basin or pan. Toss it again before serving.) For 50 or more portions, make 4 times the above amount, and you'll have plenty.

* If serving Guarneri salad with bigos (this does go well for a buffet), then omit the sausage or ham.

Lee Traub's Danish Mushroom Salad

1½ pounds fresh mushrooms, as pale and
  unblemished as possible
1 lemon

2 tablespoons mayonnaise, preferably homemade
1 clove garlic, finely minced
Salt and freshly ground pepper to taste

Wipe the mushrooms clean with a cloth or paper towels. Trim off the rough ends of the stems. Slice lengthwise into thin "umbrella" shapes. Sprinkle immediately with the juice of 1 lemon. Toss lightly but thoroughly with well-mixed mayonnaise, garlic, salt and pepper. The mixture may seem dry, but after 1 to 2 hours in the refrigerator, it will become more liquid. Stir lightly several times while chilling (for a minimum of 2 hours). Serve on dry lettuce leaves.

Lee Traub's Danish Dilled Cucumber and Bean Salad

1½ pounds fresh green beans, French cut (or two
  10-ounce packages frozen French cut beans)
2 cups sour cream
2 tablespoons finely snipped fresh dill

1 tablespoon lemon juice
2 cucumbers, sliced paper thin
Salt and pepper to taste

Cook the beans in rapidly boiling salted water until just crisp-tender. Drain, plunge immediately into cold water to arrest cooking, drain well and chill. Combine sour cream, dill, lemon juice, salt and pepper, and allow to stand at room temperature for 2 hours. Dry the cucumber slices between paper towels. Dry the beans thoroughly. Toss everything together and refrigerate for at least 4 hours.

Madhur Jaffrey's Cucumber and Tomato with Lemon Juice

1 medium-sized cucumber
1 medium-sized tomato
1 teaspoon salt
⅛ to ¼ teaspoon freshly ground black pepper
1 teaspoon roasted, ground cumin seeds

1 to 1½ tablespoons lemon juice
2 tablespoons minced Chinese parsley (coriander
  greens or cilantro)
⅛ teaspoon cayenne pepper, optional

Peel the cucumber and dice it into ¼-inch cubes. Dice the tomato as finely as the cucumber. Combine all the ingredients in a serving bowl. Mix well. Cover and refrigerate for 30 minutes.

To serve: Bring the cold serving bowl to the table. This relish can be eaten with nearly all Indian meals.

(To roast the cumin in this recipe, place desired amount of whole seeds in heavy skillet over a medium flame. Stir 2 or 3 minutes or until seeds turn a darker brown. Remove from heat. The cumin can now be ground with a mortar and pestle or with a rolling pin. It is best when freshly roasted, but you could keep it for a few days in a tightly covered jar.—From *An Invitation to Indian Cooking* by Madhur Jaffrey, published by Alfred A. Knopf.)

Anne Willan's Ratatouille for 10

2 medium eggplants (about 1 lb. each), halved and cut in ⅜-inch slices
1 pound small zucchini, cut in ½-inch slices
½ cup olive oil
3 medium onions, thinly sliced
3 red or green peppers, cored, seeded and sliced
3 cloves garlic, crushed
2 teaspoons basil

1 teaspoon thyme
1 teaspoon ground coriander
¼ teaspoon anise seed, crushed
Salt and freshly ground black pepper
4 large tomatoes, peeled, seeded and chopped, or 2 cups (1 lb.) canned tomatoes, drained and chopped
2 tablespoons chopped parsley (for sprinkling)

This recipe can easily be halved; if you double it, you will get the best results by cooking it in two casseroles or, if you use one large casserole, by cooking it in the oven at a higher heat (400°). The flavor of ratatouille improves if it is made a day or two ahead.

Sprinkle the eggplants and zucchini with salt and let them stand for 30 minutes. This draws out the liquid. Drain them, rinse with cold water and blot with paper towels. If using the oven, set it at moderately hot (375°).

In a skillet, heat 2 tablespoons oil and fry the onions until soft but not brown. Layer the onions, eggplants, zucchini and peppers in a casserole (to cook on top of the stove) or in a baking dish (to cook in the oven), sprinkling the garlic, basil, thyme, coriander, anise seed, salt and pepper between the layers. Spoon the remaining oil on top. Cover and simmer on top of the stove, or cook in the heated oven for 20 to 25 minutes. Add the tomatoes, stir well, and continue cooking 20 to 25 minutes longer or until the vegetables are tender. Do not overcook or the vegetables will become soft and unappetizing. If they produce a great deal of liquid, remove the lid for the last 15 minutes of cooking. Serve hot or cold, sprinkled with parsley. For a picnic, carry and serve in the baking dish or casserole.

Loredana Van Goethem's
Baked Pastas and Sartú

When preparing any baked pasta dish, one should make sure to undercook the pasta in boiling water in the early steps. Loredana Van Goethem suggests boiling shells or penne for only 3 or 4 minutes; however, this may result in a final product that is possibly a little too *al dente* for some tastes. To be on the safe side, boil pasta half as long as suggested on the package, draining immediately and thoroughly. Baked pasta *alla Siciliana* combines macaroni with garlicky tomato sauce, sautéed eggplant, bits of mozzarella and grated sharp cheese, such as peccorino, Romano or Parmesan, in a greased casserole. Baked "white pastas," in their most basic form, are simply layered with blankets of béchamel sauce. Here is one excellent Italian version:

Salsa Besciamella

3 tablespoons sweet butter
3 tablespoons flour
2 cups hot milk
½ teaspoon salt (or a little more, according to taste)

¼ to ½ teaspoon freshly ground white pepper
¼ teaspoon freshly grated nutmeg
1 or 2 large bay leaves
½ teaspoon powdered or crushed thyme

Melt the butter in a saucepan slowly. Sprinkle the flour into it and blend well. Bring three times to the foaming point (lifting the saucepan from the heat each time the butter-flour mixture begins to foam—you must not let it brown). Gradually stir in the milk and season with salt, pepper and nutmeg. Stir briskly with a whisk. Add bay leaf and thyme. Cook until boiling, whisking constantly. Cook 2 or 3 minutes longer, whisking, until smooth and satiny. Remove the bay leaf. If you are not ready to use the sauce immediately, dot the surface with specks of butter to form a protective film so that a "skin" will not form. This recipe yields enough to sauce a one-pound box of pasta.

When layering pasta and béchamel, reserve enough sauce to spread a ½-inch thick coat over the top. Sprinkle with a cup or so of fresh white bread crumbs mixed with a cup of grated Parmesan and dot generously with butter. At this juncture, you can store the casserole in the refrigerator overnight. Before reheating, bring to room temperature, then bake in a 375° oven for approximately 40 to 50 minutes, or until the top is golden brown (the same temperature and duration is recommended for baked "red pasta"). To make a more rich or elaborate baked white pasta, you may add slices of ham or Gruyère, sautéed mushrooms with cognac (page 188), green peas, truffles, cubed cooked chicken, slivered almonds—in short, whatever appeals to you most.

Sartú

Sartú, in the authentic Neapolitan version, is an extremely complicated timbale of rice, meats, tomatoes and cheese encased in a thick crust of layered, egg-painted bread-crumbs. An easier version is Loredana Van Goethem's: prepare rice as for risotto, omitting the saffron (page 188). Layer rice in a buttered casserole with sautéed mushrooms, undercooked peas, small chunks of cooked Italian sausage, tiny browned meatballs and grated cheese. Cover with a thin tomato purée or sauce, and top it with grated cheese. Heat in a moderate oven (325–350°) for ½ to ¾ hour, or until thoroughly heated through.

Bruce Sinclair's
Blender Pesto alla Genovese

½ cup pine nuts
⅓ cup chopped fresh basil
2 to 3 tablespoons chopped raw spinach leaves
   (optional)
2 teaspoons chopped garlic
½ cup freshly grated Foie Fiore Sardo (or ¼ cup

freshly grated Romano and ¼ cup freshly grated
Parmesan, for a somewhat less piquant flavor)
½ cup olive oil
6 to 7 tablespoons soft butter
¼ teaspoon salt
¼ teaspoon black pepper

Mix all the ingredients together well and blend. Store in the refrigerator in jars covered with a float of olive oil. With butter, keeps 7 to 10 days; substitute more oil for the butter, and it will keep under refrigeration for up to 2 months. Note: Bruce sometimes substitutes walnuts, which are less expensive and more easy to come by, for pine nuts.

Saffron Risotto with Cognac-Flamed Mushrooms alla Francesco

3 cups long-grain rice

1⅓ sticks of sweet butter (lightly salted permissible)

4 tablespoons finely minced shallots (about 18 average-sized ones)

Roughly 1 teaspoon saffron strands (two 2-gram containers will do)

1 cup Orvieto (or other good dryish Italian white wine, such as Soave)

4 cups strong homemade chicken broth (or, in a pinch, two 13¾ fl. oz. cans)

Salt and freshly ground white pepper

2 cups freshly grated Parmesan cheese (if you're positive that fresh Parmesan is unavailable, substitute an equivalent amount of ready-grated from *jars*, not cardboard tubes)

In a paella pan or large frying pan (in either case you will later need a lid), melt the butter over very low heat. Add the minced shallots, raise the heat slightly, and sauté until limp and transparent, a matter of a few minutes. Stir in the rice and cook over medium heat, coating each grain with butter and continuing to stir gently with a wooden spoon until the rice turns a golden beige and gives off a slightly toasted, nutty aroma. This should take at least 5 to 7 minutes.

Meanwhile, in a saucepan, simmer the broth and wine along with the saffron for 10 minutes. Strain cup by cup into the sautéed rice and bring briefly to a boil. Stir, cover tightly and turn the flame down to a flicker (or switch to low). If steam escapes, cover the rice with lengths of foil, tamp down around the outside of the pan and replace the lid. As rice varies, in 20 minutes check for moistness and correct seasoning with a little salt and freshly ground white pepper. If rice is still too resilient, cover for a few minutes more of slow cooking, adding a small amount, ½ cup at most, of boiling water if all the liquid has evaporated. On the other hand, if the rice seems done, but still a little too moist, remove the lid and foil and let it dry for a few minutes over low heat. Set the pan aside for the rice to cool (or transfer it to a more socially presentable ovenproof dish in which it can eventually be served). Serves 6 to 8.

Cognac-Flamed Mushrooms

2½ pounds mushrooms, halved or quartered, depending on size

5 tablespoons good fruity olive oil

1 large or 2 small cloves of garlic, finely minced

½ of a fresh grated nutmeg (about 1 teaspoon)

1 tablespoon coarse kosher salt

Freshly ground white pepper

⅓ cup cognac

In a wide frying or paella pan, bring oil almost to the smoking point over high heat. Toss the mushrooms with a wooden spoon until they squeak and begin to turn brown. Add garlic, stirring constantly. If mushrooms suddenly release a flood of juice, push them to one side, tip the pan and boil the liquid, still over a high flame, until it is substantially reduced. Continue cooking until the mushrooms turn a dark walnut shade. Sprinkle with nutmeg, season highly with white pepper and salt, lower the heat, splash on the cognac, *stand back* and ignite the juices. Toss the mushrooms until the flames subside.

When tepid, stir a cup of grated cheese into the rice, then push back toward the side of the pan into a loose ring. Arrange the mushrooms in the center cavity, sprinkle the rice with another cup of cheese and dot it with butter. Cover with foil. Do not refrigerate. To serve, heat thoroughly in a medium oven (at least 15 minutes or more) and take as is to the table or sideboard.

Geoffrey Holder's Glorified Bulljoul

2 lbs. salt cod
1½ lbs. shrimp
Juice from 2½ lemons
1 teaspoon ground black pepper
½ teaspoon dried thyme
1 large red onion
2 large bell peppers

One 10-oz. bottle of green olives
1 bunch of watercress
2 ribs of celery, chopped
2 tomatoes peeled and chopped
1 large avocado
1 cup olive oil
Lettuce leaves

Soak the salt cod overnight in cold water. The next day drain it, put it in a saucepan, and cover it with cold water. Boil for 5 minutes. Drain, remove bones, and squeeze the flesh with your hands. Shred the fish and put it in a mixing bowl. Boil the shrimp for a couple of minutes in water; shell and de-vein them and add to the cod. Add the juice of the lemons, the pepper and the thyme. Chop the onion and the peppers and stir them into the fish. Add the olives, watercress, celery and tomatoes. Peel and cube the avocado and put it in a blender. Blend it and gradually add the oil. Pour this into the fish mixture and stir it all up gently. Put the whole thing into a serving dish and garnish with lettuce and some more tomatoes and avocado if you like. (From *Geoffrey Holder's Caribbean Cookbook*, by Geoffrey Holder, published by the Viking Press.)

Ruth Spear's Striped Bass
Baked with Mussels and Shrimp

1 striped bass or weakfish, 5 pounds whole,
  cleaned and gutted, head and tail left on
Salt and fresh pepper
2 to 3 branches fresh tarragon or ½ teaspoon
  dried
Several parsley branches
6 tablespoons butter

2 medium onions, chopped
¼ pound mushrooms, sliced
¾ to 1 cup white wine
½ pound mussels, debearded and scrubbed
½ pound uncooked shrimp, shelled and de-veined
⅓ cup fresh chopped parsley
3 lemons cut in half

Preheat oven to 375°. Line a broiler pan (or baking dish large enough to hold the fish) with heavy baking foil. Set aside.

Wash and dry fish and season with salt and pepper. Stuff with tarragon and parsley branches and set aside.

Melt the butter in the baking pan, add chopped onions, stir to coat them and bake about 10 minutes or until soft. Add sliced mushrooms and wine, stir. Lay fish on top. Bake 15 minutes.

Put mussels around fish, baste both and bake 10 minutes longer. Add shrimp, baste everything again and bake another 10 minutes. At the end of the 35 minutes cooking time the mussels will be open, the shrimp pink and the fish baked through. (If using a larger fish, increase the initial baking time accordingly.)

Cover the body of the fish with chopped parsley and serve right in the baking pan, garnished with lemon halves. Serves 6.

Naomi Graffman's Interpretation
of Mrs. Artur Rubenstein's Polish Bigos

2 pounds sauerkraut
4 to 6 dried mushrooms
2 medium-sweet apples, peeled, cored and sliced
One 20-ounce can tomatoes
10 peppercorns
1 bay leaf

2 to 4 cups diced Polish sausages or a mixture of
  bratwurst, weisswurst, bauernwurst (all or any)
  or frankfurters or leftover meat such as beef,
  veal, pork or lamb
1 cup salt pork or bacon, cubed

Wash the sauerkraut in cold water and squeeze it dry.

Soak the mushrooms several hours in water to cover. Then bring to a boil and simmer until they are soft. Slice the mushrooms and add them to the sauerkraut, along with the liquid in which they were cooked. Add the tomatoes, peppercorns and bay leaf. Cover and simmer 1¼ hours.

Add the diced meats and salt pork to the sauerkraut and cook one hour longer. Serve the bigos with steamed potatoes.

At a mixed buffet, where several other dishes are offered, this is enough for 8 to 10 portions.

Marina de Brantes'
Canard aux Raisins

(from the Brantes-Autet school of French cuisine)

1 duck (4 to 5 pounds)
2 pounds green seedless grapes
4 tablespoons butter
2 tablespoons flour
2 tablespoons cognac

1 carrot
1 onion
1 bouquet garni
Salt, pepper

Preheat the oven to 350°. Wipe the cavity of the duck with paper towels. Reserve the liver, heart and neck. Salt and pepper the duck inside and out. Place the duck on a roasting rack which has been set in a roasting pan so that all the fat will eventually drip off. Leave it in the oven 2 to 3 hours or until crisp and brown.

Make a broth with the neck and heart of the duck in a small pan with two cups of water, 1 onion, 1 carrot, 1 bouquet garni of parsley, bay leaf and thyme, salt and pepper. Let it cook for ½ to 1 hour. Set it aside. In a skillet put 2 tablespoons of butter, add the liver and brown for 5 minutes. Flambé it with 2 tablespoons of cognac. Then purée the liver through a sieve or in a blender. Stem the 2 pounds of green seedless grapes. Put 1 pound in a blender, then strain; keep the juice. Peel the other grapes and blanch them (put in boiling water for two minutes). Drain them.

Make the sauce by melting 2 tablespoons of butter in a pan. Whisk in 2 tablespoons of flour, then the broth, a little at a time. Stir in the liver purée and juice of the grapes. Carve the duck; put the drained whole grapes around it. Serve with wild rice and sauce in a gravy boat. Serves 4.

Madhur Jaffrey's
Marinated Broiled Chicken

The chicken is marinated, then broiled. It could also be barbecued over charcoal.

3 to 3½ pounds chicken, preferably legs, thighs and breasts, or a whole chicken cut into serving pieces

Marinade:

2 medium-sized onions, peeled and coarsely chopped
4 cloves garlic, peeled and coarsely chopped
A piece of fresh ginger, about 1 inch long and 1 inch wide, peeled and coarsely chopped
2 to 3 fresh hot green chilies, or ¼ to ½ teaspoon cayenne pepper (optional)

1 teaspoon whole cumin seeds
1 tablespoon ground coriander
½ cup wine vinegar
½ cup olive or vegetable oil
2 teaspoons salt
⅛ teaspoon freshly ground pepper

Garnish:

Chinese parsley or Italian parsley, chopped

Combine all the ingredients for the marinade in the container of an electric blender. Blend at high speed until you have a smooth paste.

Pull off and discard the skin from the chicken pieces. Prick the chicken all over with a fork and place in a bowl. Pour marinade over chicken. Cover and refrigerate 2 to 3 hours. (24 hours would be best.)

Fifty minutes before serving, heat your broiler. Remove the chicken pieces from the bowl and, with as much marinade clinging to them as possible, place on a baking sheet lined with aluminum foil. Broil 15 minutes on each side or until the chicken gets well browned. (Adjust the distance from the broiler so it does not brown too fast.)

To serve: Place the chicken on a warm platter and sprinkle the parsley over it. Serves 4 to 6. (From *An Invitation to Indian Cooking,* by Madhur Jaffrey, published by Alfred A. Knopf.)

Ruth Spear's Stuffed Breast of Veal

A whole breast of veal can weigh from 4½ to 9 pounds, depending on the size of the animal. Ask the butcher for a piece about 3½ to 4½ pounds with a pocket for stuffing, and have him remove as many of the rib bones as possible. The amount of stuffing required will depend, of course, on the size of the breast.

1 medium onion, diced
4 tablespoons butter
1½ pounds mixed ground pork and veal
¼ cup chopped parsley
½ cup bread crumbs
Salt, freshly ground pepper

½ to 1 cup dry white wine
1 breast of veal with a pocket, 3½ to 4½ pounds
1 clove garlic, put through a press
1 teaspoon thyme
3 tablespoons cooking oil

Preheat oven to 325°.

Sauté the onions in 1 tablespoon butter until wilted. Mix with the meat, parsley, and bread crumbs and season with salt and pepper to taste. Moisten with a little white wine and stuff the pocket with the mixture. (The amount it holds will depend on the size of the breast and the pocket.) Cover the open end with a doubled piece of aluminum foil and shape it firmly to cover well. A couple of skewers may help to secure the opening.

Combine the garlic, 1 teaspoon salt, and thyme, and rub the mixture well into the breast.

Heat the remaining butter and oil and brown the breast on both sides. Then place it in the preheated oven for about 1 hour, or allow 20 minutes per pound, remembering that the stuffing is part of the weight. Baste occasionally with the pan juices.

If you plan to serve the veal hot, make a gravy as follows:

Remove the meat from the roaster pan and keep warm. Skim off any excess fat from the pan juices. In a saucepan melt 2 tablespoons butter and add 2 tablespoons flour, stirring until smoothly blended. Add pan juices and enough chicken broth to make about a cup. Correct seasoning and stir in some heavy cream.

This dish is a good traveler. Carry the meat covered in foil and the gravy in a separate jar. It can be served hot, warm, or cold. Serves 4 to 6.

Remi Saunder's Piroshki

Piroshki Dough for Meat Filling

½ pound lightly salted butter
½ pound cream cheese

2 cups sifted all-purpose flour
1 egg

Cut chilled butter and cream cheese into small bits. Sift flour into a bowl. With a pastry blender or two knives, work butter and cream cheese into the flour until coarsely mealy. At this point, you may start working the mixture with the fingertips, as lightly as possible, until it is blended into a rough dough. Divide it into two balls and squeeze each lightly between the palms until they hold their shape. Refrigerate overnight or for at least two hours. Generously flour a pastry board and rolling pin. Roll out one ball at a time to the thickness of light pie crust; if it is too thin, it will break during baking. Sprinkle it lightly with flour if the dough begins to stick to the pin. With a 3 to 3½-inch glass or round cookie cutter, cut out circles, center with a scant teaspoonful of filling, fold over and firmly crimp the edges with the fingers. Roll up excess pastry and repeat. Brush turnovers with well-beaten egg and bake at 375° until golden brown, about 20 to 25 minutes.

Piroshki Filling

The most simple meat filling can be made by sautéeing two finely chopped medium yellow onions in two tablespoons of butter and one tablespoon of oil until transparent; add 1 pound ground chuck and cook over medium heat only until tan-pink, gently break down all lumps with the back of a wooden spoon. Season with salt, pepper and a pinch of thyme. For a more distinctive filling, however, try this sausage mixture:

Sausage Piroshki Filling

1 pound fatty ground pork
3 finely minced cloves of garlic
½ cup finely chopped onion
2 tablespoons butter

1 tablespoon oil
2 teaspoons dried basil
1 teaspoon anise seed
Salt and white pepper

Sauté the garlic and onion in butter and oil until transparent. Add the pork, breaking it down with a wooden spoon, and cook over medium heat until the meat turns the color of the inside of a well-done hamburger. Add basil and anise seed, cook one minute longer and season highly with salt and pepper (it is now safe to taste). Cool and fill the pastry circles.

Helen McCully's Baked
Ham with Apricot Glaze

You have a choice of cook-before-eating hams or fully cooked hams. Whatever type you choose, Helen recommends glazing it, if only for looks. This apricot glaze is an especially easy one, used by many fine chefs.

1 8- to 10-pound ham, bone in

1 jar (12-ounce size) commercial apricot jam, not dietetic

Preheat the oven to 325° (or slow) for 15 minutes before the ham goes in the oven.

Whatever type ham, loosen the skin for about 2 inches at the shank end. Then, with scissors, make a sawtooth design around the edge. Scrape off any paper labels. Place the ham, fat side up, on the rack in the roasting pan in the preheated 325° oven and bake 3½ hours.

While the ham is baking, make the apricot glaze by placing the jar of jam *without its cover* in a small saucepan of hot water until the contents have melted. Then push the jam through a fine sieve to get rid of any pulp.

A half-hour before the ham is cooked, take it out of the oven, spoon the purée over the fat on the ham. Return the ham to the oven for the remainder of the prescribed cooking time, or until the glaze has set. Serve cold on a handsome platter; garnish with a bouquet of fresh watercress or parsley.

Ruth Spear's Barbecued Marinated Leg of Lamb

6-pound leg of lamb, boned and butterflied
1 teaspoon coarsely cracked pepper
4 cloves garlic, sliced
2 tablespoons vinegar
½ cup red wine

½ cup olive oil
2 bay leaves
½ teaspoon dried tarragon
2 tablespoons salt

Spread the lamb flat on a glass or enamel container. Sprinkle with pepper and garlic. Mix the remaining ingredients, add to the lamb and marinate in the refrigerator for 24 hours before cooking. Turn occasionally.

Remove the meat from the marinade and cook over very hot coals for 6 minutes each side. Meat should be well browned and crusty. Spread out coals to reduce intensity of heat, and continue cooking 6 to 7 minutes longer *each* side, or a total of 25 minutes. Slice as you would a steak. Serves 8.

Luisa-Esther Flynn's
Argentine Barbecue Sauce

Finely mince 2 stalks celery, 1 bunch parsley, yellow onion (to yield ⅔ cup), 2 or 3 cloves of garlic—if you like garlic—and stir into a pint of red wine vinegar. Add 3 seeded dry red pepper pods, or more, depending on how much heat you like. Pour into a bottle through a funnel and keep it in the refrigerator (lasts for several months). Bore a hole in a cork just big enough for the liquid to pass through, and stopper the bottle firmly—shake the sauce over the meat.

Carol Inouye's Yakitori Marinade

Mix together well:

½ cup saki, dry sherry or white wine
½ cup soy sauce
1 tablespoon sugar

1 crushed clove of garlic
1 teaspoon grated fresh ginger

Carol Inouye's Mixed Tempura

1 egg
1 cup sifted flour
¾ cups ice-cold water

1 teaspoon sugar
½ teaspoon baking soda

Beat the egg until slightly frothy. Slowly beat in the other ingredients until smooth. Into this batter, Carol dips shrimp, bay scallops, bite-sized chunks of fish fillets and vegetables—⅛-inch slices of yams or white potatoes, carrots sliced on the bias, 2½-inch lengths of asparagus and scallions, mushrooms, wide strips of green pepper, little bundles of green beans, parsley or carrot tops. These are fried a few pieces at a time, in deep "peanut or vegetable oil, very hot, in a wok or deep iron skillet—deep enough for the pieces of food to float without crowding." Each piece should take about three minutes to cook to a pale golden-brown. The ideal temperature for deep frying tempura is 350°; an electric deep-fryer is a splendid party accessory in that it maintains an even temperature and, as food can be cooked in a leisurely manner, guests may try their hands at it, if they like.

Remi Saunder's Paskha à la Fenja

¼ pound sweet butter
1½ cups of sugar
1 vanilla bean
1 egg yolk

2 pounds farmer's cheese, preferably in one piece
½ cup chopped blanched almonds
Optional: currants, glazed fruit and grated
  almonds

Cream butter and sugar until light and fluffy. (Add a little lemon juice, if you like lemon). Beat in the egg yolk. Split the vanilla bean, mince very finely and add to the mixture. Add the farmer's cheese, mix well with the hands, electric hand beater or mixer.

Place cheese mass in several layers of cheesecloth and place in a paskha form. (Note: the point of a paskha form is to permit liquids to accumulate and drain off through a hole at the bottom. You may improvise one using either a clean clay flower pot or a perforated plastic refrigerator food container.)

Place a weight on top of the cheesecloth-wrapped cheese mass and store in the refrigerator for a minimum of 24 hours before serving. For maximum drainage, let the paskha stand at room temperature for the first 8 to 12 hours.

Unmold and decorate with currants, glazed fruit or grated almonds if you like.

The Batterberrys' Sultan's Garden

Prepare a heavy syrup by dissolving 2 cups sugar in 1 cup water over low heat. Simmer 5 minutes and let cool. (Servings depend upon quantities and variety of fruit used.)

Grapes: Marinate 2 cups halved seeded black grapes or 2 cups halved seedless green grapes in ⅔ cup medium sherry.

Oranges: Marinate the segments of 9 naval oranges, free of all skin and pith, in ½ cup syrup and 1 tablespoon orange flower water. (Reserve the zest of 1 orange, cut into long strips.)

Pineapple: Marinate 1 ripe pineapple, cored and cut into chunks, in ¼ cup syrup and 4 tablespoons kirschwasser.

Honeydew: Marinate 1 honeydew melon, sliced into thin rindless wedges, in the juices which escape when cutting mixed with the juice of 1 lime and 1 tablespoon rose water.

Cantaloupe: Marinate 1 cantaloupe, sliced into thin rindless wedges, in ¼ cup syrup and 3 tablespoons Grand Marnier or Cointreau.

Strawberries: Marinate halved strawberries in 4 tablespoons raspberry syrup and 2 tablespoons Crème de Cassis.

Papaya: Marinate 1 ripe papaya, peeled and thinly sliced, in the juice of one lime (and a few tablespoons of syrup if necessary). Chill all fruits in separate bowls or soup plates.

Garniture: Arrange fruits in a colorful pattern on a large platter. Sprinkle the orange segments with finely chopped pistachios. Sprinkle the papaya with a few pieces of candied ginger, finely chopped with an oiled knife. Cut reserved orange zest into fine julienne, blanch, strain, poach in syrup for 5 minutes, drain on paper towels, and strew over melon slices. For a real tour de force, pass a bowl of sherried walnuts (page 202) to nibble with Sultan's Garden.

The Batterberrys' Pear Sorbet

Juice of 1 lemon, strained
6 large, ripe Bartlett pears
5 tablespoons sugar
3 tablespoons water

3 tablespoons pear brandy
Good pinch of salt
Good pinch of powdered ginger
3 egg whites

Pour the lemon juice into a large nonmetallic mixing bowl. Using a swivel-bladed paring knife, peel the pears, core and cut into cubes, one at a time. Then mix with the lemon juice to ward off discoloration.

Combine the sugar and water in a small saucepan. Place over medium heat. Stir until it dissolves. Cool. Add to the pears, along with the pear brandy, salt and ginger. Purée the mixture in an electric blender or food processor. Spoon into two ice-cube trays and place in the freezer. When the purée has congealed to a mush, spoon into a cold bowl and beat mercilessly with a wire whisk.

Beat the egg whites until they hold firm, shiny peaks when the beater is held straight up. Pour the purée over the whites and fold in with a rubber spatula. Whip again and return to the ice trays. After another hour, whip again and pack into a six-cup ring mold. Cover with foil, return to the freezer until firm.

To serve, place in the refrigerator for about 20 minutes to soften slightly, then unmold on a chilled platter or plate. Garnish with sprigs of fresh mint or pitted black cherries, macerated in kirsch with possibly a dash of superfine sugar. Serves 6 to 8.

Lee Traub's Mother's Schaum Torte

8 whites of eggs (approximately 1 cup)
¼ teaspoon cream of tartar
½ teaspoon salt

1 tablespoon vinegar
1 teaspoon vanilla
2 cups of sugar

Add the salt to the whites and beat until foamy. Add the cream of tartar and continue to beat until stiff, adding the vinegar and vanilla very gradually toward the end. Add the sugar *very* slowly, beating constantly (this cannot be overbeaten!).

Spoon into an 8-inch spring form which has been greased on the bottom only. Bake 1 hour at 275°. Cool. Slice in half horizontally, making two layers, and fill and cover with whipped cream and one of following:

Berries
Toasted chopped nuts
Shaved chocolate and pieces of marron glacé
Orange peel which has been cooked in heavy syrup

Decorate the outside with whipped cream and candied slices of orange.

Coffee Cup Soufflé

(A Recipe from The Four Seasons)

4½ tablespoons butter
4½ tablespoons flour
1½ cups milk
6 eggs

3 tablespoons instant coffee
¾ cup sugar
4 tablespoons coffee ice cream

Mix the flour with the butter until all the flour is absorbed. Place the milk in a saucepan and bring to a boil. Add the butter-flour mixture and stir until thick. Cool. Separate the eggs and add the yolks and coffee to the original mixture. Beat the egg whites until they form soft peaks. Continue beating, gradually adding the sugar, until they form stiff peaks. Fold into the yolk mixture. Set aside 4 tablespoons of the soufflé mixture. Butter the insides of 6 ovenproof coffee cups and sprinkle lightly with sugar. Divide the remaining mixture between the prepared coffee cups. Bake in a 425° oven for about 11 minutes. (This will turn out a soufflé of medium consistency. Shorten or lengthen baking time a few minutes if a softer or firmer consistency is desired.) Serve with a sauce made by mixing the reserved soufflé mixture with the coffee ice cream. Serves 6.

Ruth Spear's Fresh Raspberry Pie

2 tablespoons "Minute" tapioca
1⅓ cups sugar
4 cups fresh raspberries
½ cup flour
1 teaspoon cinnamon

4 tablespoons butter
Unbaked 9-inch pastry shell
Confectioner's sugar
Whipped cream

Preheat oven to 450°.

Combine the tapioca with ⅔ cup sugar and gently mix with the raspberries. Allow to sit for 15 minutes. Combine the remaining sugar with the flour and cinnamon. Cut in the butter with a pastry blender until the mixture is crumbly. Spread the berry mixture in the pie shell. Cover with crumbs. Bake in a preheated oven for 10 minutes. Reduce heat to 350° and bake another 30 minutes, or until the crust and topping are golden. Allow the pie to cool completely. Dust with confectioner's sugar and serve with whipped cream.

The De Brantes Children's Chocolate Mousse

8 eggs
8 ounces semisweet chocolate

2 tablespoons sugar per egg

Chop the chocolate into small pieces. Melt them in a small bowl placed in a pan with hot water over a low fire, until it forms a syrup. Turn off heat. In the meantime separate egg whites from yolks. In a bowl combine the yolks with the sugar and stir with a wooden spoon until this mixture is creamy and forms bubbles. Slowly add the warm chocolate—stirring constantly. Beat the egg whites into stiff peaks and fold slowly into the chocolate—lifting the mixture from the bottom to blend it well.

Spoon into tiny chocolate pots and refrigerate at least 10 hours. Serve with heavy or unsweetened whipped cream. Serves 8.

The Reeds' Chocolate Meringue Cookies

Melt a 6-ounce package of Nestlé's semisweet chocolate bits in the top of a double boiler. Beat 2 egg whites with a pinch of salt until foamy. Gradually add ½ cup of sugar while still beating. Add ¼ teaspoon of vanilla extract and ¼ teaspoon cream of tartar. Continue beating until stiff but not breaking apart. Fold in the melted chocolate and ¾ cup of chopped walnuts. Drop by teaspoons onto a buttered cookie sheet. Bake 8 to 10 minutes in a 350° oven. Remove instantly from the sheet—or else they may stick. Cool in a rack.

Worldly Sundaes

There are two principal spectrums of flavors from which to choose toppings: fruit or the almond-coffee-chocolate-mint range.

Within the fruit spectrum try a little:

Crème de Cassis: a few spoonfuls over a mélange of strawberries, raspberries and blueberries, the whole cascaded over a scoop of French vanilla ice cream or raspberry ice.

Cointreau and **Grand Marnier:** these orange-based liqueurs go equally well with vanilla ice cream or with orange segments and chopped candied orange peel over lemon or orange ice.

Poire: over pear sorbet (page 198).

Cherry Heering: over cranberry ice.

Apricot Brandy: over pineapple ice.

Within the richer, darker range, you might experiment with:

Kahlúa: over chocolate, chocolate chip, mocha or nut ice creams.

Minted Chocolate Liqueur: over vanilla, mint or chocolate chip.

Crème de Menthe: over vanilla or chocolate chip.

Crème de Cacao: over vanilla, chocolate, coffee or rum raisin.

Amaretto di Saronno: over burnt almond, vanilla or butter crunch.

Bloomingdale's Pound Cake
(from the Delicacies Department)

1 cup butter
2 cups sugar
4 eggs
2 teaspoons vanilla

1 cup milk
3 tablespoons baking powder
3 scant cups flour

Preheat the oven to 350°. Grease a 10-inch tube pan. Beat the ingredients together, adding one at a time. Pour half of the batter into the tube pan and mix together the following:

1½ ounces baking chocolate, melted
A pinch of baking soda

2 tablespoons milk
2 tablespoons remaining batter mix

Cut this second mixture into the batter in the tube pan and add the remaining batter. Bake 45 minutes or until done.

Bloomingdale's Whole Grain Muffins
(from "Forty Carrots")

2 cups whole wheat flour
⅛ teaspoon salt
¼ cup nonfat powdered milk
3 tablespoons baking powder

1 cup bran
¼ cup oil
⅓ cup honey
1 cup milk

Sift together the flour, salt, powdered milk and baking powder. Add the remaining ingredients and mix. Bake in muffin tins at 400° for 12 to 15 minutes. Yield: 12 muffins.

The Batterberrys' Homemade Candies

Sherried Walnuts

Boil 1½ cups granulated sugar with ½ cup medium sherry until the "soft ball" stage is reached (234–240° on a candy thermometer). Remove from heat and stir in 3 cups of

202

English walnuts and ½ teaspoon of cinnamon. Continue stirring until cloudy, a matter of a few minutes. Turn out into a buttered pan and rapidly separate the nuts from each other with two forks. Store in a tight container.

Apricot Sugarplums

Rind of a navel orange
11-ounce package of dried apricots
1 cup granulated sugar

¼ cup orange juice
1 cup coarsely crushed pecans

Chop the rind and apricots finely (or grind coarsely). Add the sugar and orange juice. Cook in the top of a double boiler, stirring occasionally, at least half an hour—the mixture should become stiff. Remove from heat, cool and add chopped nuts. Combine well. Shape into small bars (about "two-bites" size) with wet hands. Roll in granulated sugar. Apricot sugarplums may be made several weeks in advance. Store them in an airtight container with sheets of waxed paper between each layer. If the apricot sugarplums become slightly sticky, roll them all up in granulated sugar once again before serving.

A Splendid Repertoire of Drinks

To assemble this up-to-the-minute list, we have solicited the impeccable advice of the custodians of four of the world's greatest bars.

From the "21" Club come the vital statistics on three of their best-known classics:

"21" 's Bloody Mary

Pour 1½ ounces of vodka into an ice-filled cocktail shaker. Add 4 ounces of tomato juice, dashes of pepper, salt, Worcestershire sauce and celery salt, and ½ ounce freshly squeezed lemon juice. Shake lightly and pour over rocks into a stemmed glass.

"21"'s Whiskey Sour

Mix 1½ teaspoons of honey with the juice of 1 lemon. Pour into a shaker filled with ice, add 2½ ounces of blended whiskey, shake well and pour over rocks into a stemmed glass.

"21"'s Dry Martini

Pour 2½ ounces of gin and ¼ ounce of dry vermouth over ice. Stir gently until well chilled and pour into a stemmed cocktail glass.

From the Plaza come three aristocratic traditions and one Polynesian powerhouse:

The Plaza's Black Velvet

Simultaneously pour 1 part chilled Guinness Stout to 1 part chilled champagne into a 10-ounce Pilsner glass. Do not stir.

The Plaza's Champagne Cocktail

Place 1 cube of sugar in the center of a chilled champagne glass. Sprinkle 3 drops of Angostura bitters on the cube. Fill the glass with chilled champagne, approximately 4½ ounces.

The Plaza's Ramos Gin Fizz

Combine ½ ounce of rock candy syrup, 1 ounce of lemon juice, 2 ounces of fresh milk, 1 egg white, 3 dashes of orange flower water (available at pharmacies), 1 ounce of gin. Shake strenuously with ice cubes until extremely frothy. Strain into a chilled fizz or wine glass.

Trader Vic's Fog Cutter

Shake 2 ounces of gold rum (preferably Trader Vic's), ½ ounce of gin, 1 ounce of orange juice, 2 ounces of lemon juice, ½ ounce of orgeat syrup with cracked ice. Pour into a tall glass with ice and top with a float of sherry. Serve with straws.

From the magnificently avant-garde bar of The Four Seasons we learn of favorites old and new:

The Four Seasons' British Lion

Into a shaker over ice pour 2 ounces of Grand Marnier, 1 ounce of fresh lime juice and a dash of grenadine. Shake well and strain into a cocktail glass.

The Four Seasons' Ancient Martini

Pour ¼ ounce of Noilly Prat vermouth, 2¾ ounces of Beefeater gin and a dash of Grand Marnier over ice. Stir and serve in a cocktail glass. Garnish with lemon peel.

The Four Seasons' Tequila Grape or Tequila Apple

In a highball glass, over ice, pour 2 ounces of tequila and add 6 ounces of grapefruit or apple juice.

The Four Seasons' Suffering Bastard

Pour ¾ ounce of gin, ¾ ounce of brandy, 1 teaspoon of bitters, and teaspoon of Rose's lime juice into a tall highball glass and stir. Add ice cubes and ½ pint of ginger ale. Decorate with lemon and orange slices and a sprig of mint.

For after-dinner drinks, what better source than the legendary Hotel Algonquin, where the bar, lobby and dining room, in the tradition of decades, are nightly crowded with imbibing theatergoers and semiresident celebrities in the arts. On a year-round basis, we are told, people seem to be veering toward "simpler, less frigid after-dinner drinks than in the past—the kind one can stay with easily during long conversation. The stand-out favorite is a good tall Scotch and plain water, with little or no ice. It's mellower, softer to drink it this way; you don't chill the flavor out of the whiskey. Also, chilled, but not ice-cold, white wines are becoming very popular—a full-bodied Sauterne, a fruity Rhine, a dry Chablis. Many are even ordering Kir, something of a switch for a drink that the French have always served as an apértif. Of course, there are those who are still faithful to brandy or who order a fine Port or vintage Madeira after dinner, sometimes enhancing the aroma with a snifter. Or on cold nights, many like to warm up with an Irish Coffee, or a Bull Shot, steaming hot."

Kir (Vin Blanc Cassis) à la Algonquin

In a stemmed wine glass with a twist of lemon, add a dash of Crème de Cassis (currant liqueur) to an average serving of chilled dry white wine (note: a good jug wine can be used).

The Algonquin's Hot Bull Shot

Into a warmed 8-ounce mug pour 1½ ounces of vodka and 6 ounces of hot beef bouillon. Spice with a double dash of Worcestershire sauce, a drop of Tabasco, and freshly ground pepper. Top off with a wafer-thin slice of lemon, and serve steaming hot.

The Algonquin's Irish Coffee

Into a stemmed 6- or 8-ounce glass pour 1 jigger of Irish whiskey. Fill the glass to within a half-inch of the brim with black coffee—hot and strong. Add sugar to taste and stir well. Top off with lightly whipped cream so that the cream floats on top.

Geoffrey Holder's
Snake Bite Rum Punch

1½ cups sugar
2 cups lemon juice
8 cups dry white wine
2 quarts light or dark rum
½ teaspoon bitters

1 cup maraschino cherries
1½ cups diced fresh fruit
2 cups canned or fresh pineapple
Orange slices for garnish

Combine all the ingredients except for the orange slices in a large punch bowl, and put it in the freezer overnight. One hour before your guests arrive, remove the bowl from the freezer and garnish with the orange. Mr. Holder uses only Jamaica, Trinidad or Barbados rum—Vat 19, Old Oak, Mount Gay or Myers. "Dark rum," he advises, "like brown sugar, is best. When you open up a bottle of rum it should smell like sugar cane."

A Party Punch With
or Without Spirits

Punch base: Brew 1 quart of very strong tea (Orange Pekoe, Darjeeling or a combination of the two) to which has been added a scant palmful of dried mint leaves. Steep for 10 minutes. Strain into an enamel saucepan. Sweeten with at least 1 cup of bottled raspberry syrup. Heat to the simmering point, stir well, and while it is still hot, pour it over 4 thinly sliced juice oranges and 4 sliced lemons (which, earlier, were generously sprinkled with superfine sugar and left to macerate in a nonmetallic bowl for at least 2 hours). Stir until any lingering grains of sugar are dissolved.

For punch with spiritous authority, add a 4/5 bottle of golden rum and a cup of cognac. For non-alcoholic punch, add nothing. In either case, cover tightly and store in a cool place (or refrigerator) for 24 to 48 hours.

When ready to use, discard the exhausted fruit and proceed:

For non-alcoholic punch, pour the punch base over a block or large chunks of ice in a transparent punch bowl. Add ½ cup of fresh lemon juice, 1 quart of orange juice, 1 quart of cranberry juice, 1 quart of ginger ale, and three slight dashes of Angostura bitters. Taste. As the acidity of fruit juices tends to vary, it may be necessary to correct the flavor, in which case, gradually stir in more raspberry syrup until desired sweetness is achieved.

Decorate with navel oranges and lemons, thinly sliced and seeded, and a small box of rinsed whole strawberries.

Make 26 to 28 medium punch cups.

For the tea-rum-cognac-based punch, add only the lemon juice plus 3 bottles of dry white wine, 1 quart of club soda, and 3 slight dashes of Angostura bitters.

Again, if needed, correct the sweetness with raspberry syrup. Decorate with sliced oranges and lemons and, if you have the time and inclination, with a cubed and sugared fresh pineapple which has been marinating in kirschwasser.

Makes about 36 servings.

Bloomingdale's
"Pick Me Upper" Milk Shakes

(from "Forty Carrots")

Sunshine Shake

4 ounces cantaloupe chunks
5 ounces skim milk
1 tablespoon honey

2 ice cubes or 2 ounces chopped ice
1 tablespoon plain yogurt

Combine all the ingredients in a blender and whip. Makes one 12-ounce serving.
To prepare a Pink Cloud, substitute 4 ounces of frozen raspberries for the cantaloupe.
To prepare a Banana Whisk, substitute 4 ounces of fresh banana for the cantaloupe.